DECORATING WITH PLANTS

DECORATING WITH PLANTS

WHAT TO CHOOSE, WAYS TO STYLE, AND HOW TO MAKE THEM THRIVE

BAYLOR CHAPMAN

Photographs by Aubrie Pick

ARTISAN | NEW YORK

Also by Baylor Chapman
The Plant Recipe Book

Library of Congress Cataloging-in-Publication Data

Names: Chapman, Baylor, author.
Title: Decorating with plants / Baylor Chapman ; photographs by Aubrie Pick.
Description: New York : Artisan, a division of
Workman Publishing Co., Inc. [2019] | Includes index.
Identifiers: LCCN 2018030427 | ISBN 9781579657765 (hardcover : alk. paper)
Subjects: LCSH: House plants in interior decoration. | House plants.
Classification: LCC SB419.25 .C45 2019 | DDC 635.9/65—dc23LC record
available at https://lccn.loc.gov/2018030427

Design by Jennifer K. Beal Davis
Endpaper illustration by Matt Davis

Artisan books are available at special discounts when purchased in bulk for
premiums and sales promotions as well as for fund-raising or educational use.
Special editions or book excerpts also can be created to specification. For details,
contact the Special Sales Director at the address below, or send an e-mail to
specialmarkets@workman.com.

For speaking engagements, contact speakersbureau@workman.com.

Published by Artisan
A division of Workman Publishing Co., Inc.
225 Varick Street
New York, NY 10014-4381
artisanbooks.com

Artisan is a registered trademark of Workman Publishing Co., Inc.

Published simultaneously in Canada by Thomas Allen & Son, Limited

Printed in China

3 5 7 9 10 8 6 4 2

*To my parents,
to whom I'll be forever
grateful for encouraging all of
my plant-related pursuits*

CONTENTS

PART I: THE GO-TO PLANT LIST

PART II: A ROOM-BY-ROOM GUIDE

INTRODUCTION

When your house is an expression of what you love, it makes you feel at home. Whether you're in a short-term apartment rental or a long-lived-in bungalow, personal touches are what make a place *yours*. Along with furniture, artwork, and decor, plants are a wonderful way to communicate your style and add "soul" to a space. When you get right down to it, plants bring a breath of fresh air to your rooms like nothing else can. Here are just a few things that houseplants can do for you and your home.

Strike a mood. By bridging the indoors and outdoors and reinforcing our connection to nature, plants encourage us to slow down and settle in. This often happens at a subconscious level: we may not be immediately aware of plants' calming effect, but it's there.

Set a tone. Delicate flowers communicate a soft, feminine touch, while a structural, dark-hued plant offers an edgier, more modern vibe. An oddball plant, in contrast, will reveal your flair for the curious and cool.

Define a space. Plants can be arranged to direct the eye. They can lead people into or out of a space or create a barrier or "wall" to make one room seem like two.

Clean the air. Plants scrub the air in their immediate surroundings by taking in harmful toxins, processing them in their leaves and through the soil, and releasing clean air into the environment. Plants even remove particulate matter such as dust, pollen, and pollution. (Turn to page 188 to learn about especially impressive purifiers.)

Mitigate sound. Plants soak up, buffer, and generally dampen noise. The sizable leaves of the fiddle-leaf fig, for example, absorb sound waves, while feathery palm fronds will diffract them.

Generate an aroma. Fragrant blooms and leaves can subtly define a space, soothing or energizing those who dwell in it. (Turn to page 102 for some of my favorite aromatic plants.)

I love plants so much that I've spent more than fifteen years surrounding myself with them. In that time, I founded Lila B., a San Francisco–based, green-certified plant and flower design business; authored my first book, *The Plant Recipe Book*; and turned a parking lot in the middle of San Francisco into a garden. At the heart of it all has been my belief that no matter where you live, you can enjoy a little bit of green.

Whether you crave a bit of nature but don't know where to start or you already have a bunch of plants but want to arrange them in a more stylish, composed, or thoughtful way, this book is here to help. Filled with design tips, care info, and a whole lot more, the pages that follow will provide you with the tools and inspiration you need to decorate with plants. Replicate one of the looks featured here, or use the design principles and plant knowledge in these pages to create a style all your own.

Part I of the book will introduce you to my go-to houseplants, specimens that are guaranteed to provide a big impact but don't have fussy care requirements. These superstars will continue to appear as I take you room by room through the home in part II. And for those of you who are already plant aficionados, you'll find plenty of out-of-the-ordinary plants tucked throughout the book, too.

Whatever plants you choose, remember these three tenets: First, you don't need to fill your entire house with plants. Just one plant that makes you smile is plenty! Research has shown that even a single flower can improve your mood, and a single plant can significantly clean the air. Second, there's no such thing as a "black thumb." Sure, some people seem to have a natural gift with plants, but everyone can learn how to care for them. Observe your plants carefully, and they'll tell you what they need (you'll

learn more about these visual clues in "Caring for Your Plant" beginning on page 20). Tend to them as best you can, and if one doesn't make it, try, try, and try again, until you find one that suits you, your lifestyle, and your home. And third, go ahead and break the design rules. Scale, color, light, texture, and balance . . . these elements all work together to create a harmonious space, but you needn't be rigid about how you apply them. Move things around until you like how they look. Can't find the perfect spot for a new plant? Give it to a friend!

I am excited to join you on this journey to bring more plants into your home, and eager for you to reap the benefits that they provide. One plant may brighten your space with its beauty while another soothes your sunburns (thanks, aloe!)—and you may find that the relationship you develop with your plant companions is actually the most gratifying benefit of all. Some plants will require you to tend to them more than others, but they are worth every bit of time and effort. Plants are magical and can instantly turn any house into a home.

GETTING STARTED

Nuts and bolts. The foundation. Plants 101. Whatever you'd like to call it, the following pages cover the basic information you'll need to know as you begin to bring plants into your home. Some of these tips will be helpful before you even pick out your first green companion, while other instructions may come in handy months down the road when you're in need of some plant SOS. Feel free to skip ahead to parts I and II to get an idea of *what* appeals, then come back here for the nitty-gritty. Whether you're ready to grab a plant and get rolling or just looking for an idea of what it will be like to live with plants, this section is here to help.

CHOOSING AND BUYING YOUR PLANT

Before you can design with plants, you need the plants themselves. Plant nurseries, boutique plant stores, and garden centers have trained experts on hand to answer your questions and guide you in taking home the right specimen. There are plenty of other places to pick up plants, too, such as grocery outlets, hardware stores, craft shops, and flower stands. If you'd rather shop from home, online plant retailers, as well as sites such as Etsy, offer a ton of options, including hard-to-find rarities (for a few of my favorite sources, see page 264). Before you head to the store (or the Web), consider these five questions.

1. **Which room do you want the plant to live in, and what is the environment in that space?** What's the light level? Temperature range? Relative humidity? If you have your heart set on a finicky specimen that won't thrive in your space's existing conditions, you can always add "sunlight" with grow lights (see page 117) or create a more humid microclimate by placing a gravel tray under your pot (see page 24)—but know that maintaining this special mini environment will require more time and effort than choosing a plant that's naturally well suited to the room.

2. **What's your style?** Nature's original decor, plants come in a range of "styles" that can complement the rest of a room's look. Do you want something sleek, or do you crave a wild and untamed mass? Do you like vibrant colors, or would you prefer to stick to a neutral palette of greens? What do you already own that the plant would go nicely with?

3. **How big do you want it to be?** Are you looking for a floor plant or something pint-size for your desk? Ask your local nursery about the

growth rate of the plant. Monstera, for example, is a rapid grower; if you take one home, be prepared to offer it a space where it can spread its long stems, aerial roots, and oversize leaves. Others, like the ZZ plant, will take years to mature.

4. **What's your budget?** Plants, like anything else, vary in price depending on availability, season, location, and growth rate. Choose what works for you and your wallet. The smaller a plant, the cheaper it tends to be. If you are willing to be patient, you might choose a medium-size plant and simply wait for it to grow up into the floor plant of your dreams. (There's another benefit to raising your plant versus buying it full-size straightaway: growing it to maturity in your home results in a stronger plant, one that doesn't undergo the stress of acclimating from its previous environment in a nursery or shop to its new spot in your home.)

5. **How much time do you want to spend caring for your greenery?** Some plants require much more effort than others. If keeping track of when to water, mist, and fertilize makes your head spin, choose from the many houseplants that are relatively low maintenance. (See part I, beginning on page 32, for some of my favorite easy-care options.)

WHAT TO LOOK FOR WHEN BUYING A PLANT

Maybe you've found the exact plant that is on your wish list, or perhaps you've stumbled upon one and decided it just has to go home with you! Before you pull out your wallet, though, pause and take a closer look. To ensure that you're bringing home the best possible specimen, spend a few minutes with your new prospect. Touch it, pick it up, and flip over the leaves. (It's kind of like looking under the hood when you're car shopping.) Here are a few things to check out.

The Leaves: If the plant is supposed to be green, make sure the leaves are actually green, not yellow or brown. Are they bushy? Full of life? Avoid plants with wilting or torn leaves, as well as ones with notched or nibbled leaves, both signs of bugs.

The Grow Pot: You want a plant that is proportionally the correct size for its current grow pot—not too large, not too small. The roots should loosely fill the pot. Lift the pot and check the bottom: are roots growing out of the drainage holes? If so, the plant may be undesirably "root-bound." Also called "pot-bound," this is when roots are itching to grow but are tightly constrained to the pot—they keep wrapping and wrapping over themselves to create a tightly knit web of roots. If you were to *gently* lift the plant out of the grow pot, the soil should generally hold together (as shown opposite), not instantly fall apart or come out as a solid mass of roots (though you won't be able to perform this test before buying, unless you ask the garden center staff to help you).

The Buds: If flowers are what you're after, look for ripe buds, not fully open blooms. This way you can enjoy all the stages of the plant's growth.

GETTING YOUR PLANT HOME

You want your new plant to thrive in its new home; give it a leg up before you even leave the store. As insulation against cold temperatures, and to protect its leaves from unwanted bumps and bruises on even a mild day, a houseplant should be wrapped in paper (the salesperson should be able to do this for you). Bubble Wrap works well to both cushion the plant from damage and insulate it on cold winter days (you may need to bring your own). Hot weather can do just as much damage as cold, so don't leave a plant in a hot car longer than necessary.

When you get it home, unwrap your new plant and place it on a plate or tray to protect the surface underneath. If you can't get to repotting it right away (see page 15), leave it to acclimate in a draft-free and not-too-sunny place until you're ready to transplant it.

WHAT'S IN A NAME?

Every plant has two names: its Latin botanical name and its common name. Think of the botanical name as a bar code for plants—no two are the same. In contrast, plants can have multiple common names, and some common names are shared by multiple plants, which can definitely lead to confusion! That's why in part I, I include both common and botanical names—so that you can track down the exact plant that tickles your fancy. For a complete list of plants mentioned in this book by common and botanical names, turn to the appendix on page 259.

MATCHING YOUR PLANT WITH THE RIGHT SOIL

All terrestrial houseplants (see "No Soil? No Problem!" below) require a potting mix of some kind—a combination of mediums such as soil, peat, sand, perlite, leaf mold, and bark. Potting mixes are distinguished from outdoor ground soil not only by their light or "fluffy" quality, which provides air gaps that give plants access to oxygen, but also by the assured absence of any soilborne maladies.

Below are a few common potting mix options. For the majority of houseplants, regular potting mix is just fine. Check out the specifications in the Go-To Plant List beginning on page 32 or talk to your local nursery expert to get advice on a good match.

Regular Potting Mix: For most houseplants, this is the "go-to" blend—just scoop it right out of the bag and you're ready to pot (although one can certainly amend this growing medium to add more nutrients, allow for better drainage or water retention, etc.). Not all regular potting mixes are the same, but they normally feature a combination of organic and inorganic materials that are meant to hold moisture, provide nutrition, anchor roots, and offer "fluff" for aeration. Uncontaminated soil is often, but not always, an ingredient. Organic materials, derived from once-living matter, are included for moisture retention, while inorganic matter (like tiny rocks and sand) helps the mix drain. Check the label if, like me, you want to be sure to keep things natural—some mixes include artificial materials or chemical fertilizer.

Cactus Mix: This mix contains more sand and other grit like vermiculite and perlite than regular potting mix to help water drain. Because it holds less moisture than regular potting mix, it's a better option for plants that like things dry, like succulents.

Peat Moss Mix: Surprisingly, not all potting mixes include soil. Peat-based mixes work well for bromeliads and are sometimes combined with other mediums to formulate a special "violet mix," which is suitable for African violets as well as Cape primroses. Peat is a decomposed matter that originates in bog habitats. It is lightweight and excellent at retaining both water and nutrients, but unfortunately, it is not sustainable. Coir and other more sustainable materials can be substituted for peat moss as they have similar water-retaining properties. Note that these mixes are often lightweight and can't support a tall, heavy plant.

Orchid Bark: This mix of bark is formulated for plants that grow on trees, not in soil (see "No Soil? No Problem!" below). The bark chunks provide a surface for gripping as well as air gaps for the plant's roots to breathe. Some orchid mixes include leaf mold, perlite, sphagnum moss, and other ingredients. Note: Orchids are often planted and sold in sphagnum moss, making them easier to transport (no loose bits of bark!) from the grower to the retail store to your home. If the moss dries out, soak it in water for a few minutes to ensure that it absorbs enough moisture.

NO SOIL? NO PROBLEM!

Not all plants need soil to live. Those that do are called terrestrial; those that don't and instead grow on top of other plants or on outcrops are called epiphytes. Common epiphytes include air plants and some types of orchids, which latch onto tree branches to live harmoniously with their host. Other epiphytes, like mistletoe, grow parasitically on trees and damage their hosts.

POTTING YOUR PLANT

Once you get your plant home, you have a few options. You can "stage" the plant in its original grow pot, repot it in a vessel of your choosing, or do something even more creative, such as turning it into a kokedama (see page 18).

STAGING

The cleanest and easiest potting method is to "stage" your plant by keeping it in its grow pot (the original, usually plastic, container) and concealing this unattractive vessel in a cachepot (decorative container). After choosing your cachepot and ensuring that it's large enough to cover the original grow pot, insert a waterproof liner to protect against water leakage or seepage (do this even if your cachepot lacks a drainage hole). Plastic liners are available from florists or garden centers, or you can make your own by using a bowl, the cut-off bottom of a plastic bottle, or even a layer of plastic garbage bags. Make sure this liner is wider than the grow pot and is able to catch any water that drips from the sides of the pot as well as the bottom. If the grow pot sits too far down inside the cachepot, create a "riser" by adding waterproof stuffing (like Bubble Wrap), a layer of gravel, a block of wood, a large stone, or a second, upside-down grow pot to prop the plant up to the ideal height. An added benefit of a riser is that it will act as a protective spacer, keeping the plant's roots from sitting in a pool of water in the event that you accidentally overwater.

The plant staging supplies pictured here include (clockwise from far left): cork to protect the tabletop, small stones to serve as a decorative topper, a waterproof liner, Red Velvet echeveria, a saucer, a cachepot, and a large stone used to raise the grow pot to the needed height.

REPOTTING

To repot your plant, choose a pot that is roughly the same size or slightly larger than the grow pot (a small plant's root system can't reach all areas of moisture in a big pot of soil, thus leaving the soil soggy and causing the roots to rot). A pot with a drainage hole is best, as it prevents water from pooling at the bottom of the pot and suffocating the roots. If you choose a nondraining vase, be careful and sparing when watering to avoid this. Then follow the steps below.

1. Cover the drainage hole with a permeable layer, such as a piece of wire mesh (like from a window screen) or a coffee filter, to prevent soil from escaping. A curved, broken pot shard will work, too. A layer of gravel is not needed for drainage.

2. If the new pot is larger than your grow pot, add a layer of soil to the bottom of the pot. (See page 14 to learn how to choose the right potting mix.)

3. Gently tip the plant on its side, give the grow pot a squeeze, and remove the plant from the pot. Gently massage the roots to separate them (see opposite; this allows them to loosen and grow outside the shape of the original container).

4. Set the plant in its new pot. The base of the stem should rest just below the rim of the pot. Fill in with soil and give the plant a little shimmy to work the soil into all the nooks and crannies. Add more soil if needed. The soil line should rest just below the rim of the pot.

5. Cover the soil with a pretty, decorative topper. Options include moss; rocks, gravel, or pebbles; wood chips; creeping wire vine; and Spanish moss. For something out of the ordinary, try buttons, sea glass, or broken terra-cotta. (A topper is like a swept floor—it makes for a more polished look, even if you can't put your finger on why!)

6. Put something between the pot and your chosen surface—a piece of cork, a dish, a pot holder—to add one more layer of protection against water damage.

TOPDRESSING

Every year or two, your plants will benefit from a repotting. For plants that are large or prickly, or that do best with tighter roots, like a hoya, simply remove the top layer of potting mix (and any decorative topping) and add a fresh layer of soil.

Pictured here is a 'Needlepoint' dracaena, finished with a natural "carpet" of sheet moss.

KOKEDAMA

From the Japanese (*koke* means "moss" and *dama* means "ball"), a *kokedama* is a plant that is placed in a mixture of clay, peat, and soil, then wrapped with sheet moss to create a living vase. Ferns, peperomia, and ivy plants are all good candidates for kokedama. Follow the steps below to create your own.

Once your kokedama is completed, you can place it in a bowl atop tiny stones, on a tray, or in a soap dish (see page 230), or hang it from a string. Or, for a lower-maintenance setup, tuck your little moss friend on top of soil in a planted arrangement. It may just root right through its thin moss wrap! Note: Japanese clay is available online and at specialty bonsai nurseries, but it can be expensive and hard to find. In a pinch, substitute a clay or clay loam soil.

What You'll Need:

- 1 small bowl
- ½ cup (170 g) Japanese clay
- ½ cup (170 g) peat
- 1 cup (240 ml) warm water
- 8-inch (20 cm) square of sheet moss
- 1 spray bottle filled with water (optional)
- One 12-inch (30 cm) plate
- One 12-inch (30 cm) square of cellophane or foil
- 1 plant in a 4-inch (10 cm) grow pot (choose one that likes low or average light, for compatibility with moss); pictured here is an arrowhead plant
- Rubber bands
- Garden snips or scissors
- Twine

1. Mix the clay and peat in a small bowl, add the warm water a little at a time, and massage to create a thick consistency. Set aside to allow the water to be absorbed, and massage again. Spray or soak the moss with water to moisten, prevent dust, and make it more malleable. Set aside. Layer the plate with cellophane. Scoop the clay mixture onto the cellophane and make a pancake about ¼ inch (6 mm) thick and 8 inches (20 cm) across.

2. Unpot your plant, remove excess soil (to keep the moss ball in scale with the plant), and set the root ball on top of the clay pancake.

3. As if you're wrapping a gift in cellophane, enclose the soil with the clay, leaving the plant exposed. Create a ball shape with the clay. Let any extra water drain onto the cellophane. Remove the cellophane to expose the intact clay ball shape. Set aside the plant, and clean the cellophane.

4. With the green side down, lay the moss on the cellophane. Set the plant's clay ball in the center of the moss. Repeat the gift wrap movement with moss.

5. Wrap the ball with rubber bands to temporarily secure the moss. Tidy the moss, trimming around the base of the plant. Secure the moss with twine by wrapping it gently yet securely around the moss to form a ball shape. Tie off the twine or tuck it near the stem. Snip the rubber bands and remove them.

6. Keep out of direct sun, mist often, and soak in a bowl of water occasionally. Give the ball a gentle squeeze before returning it to its vessel—it shouldn't sit in a pool of water all day.

CARING FOR YOUR PLANT

Think of your plant as a friend—an exceptional creature in its own right that drinks water, needs nutrients, craves light, breathes air, and even sleeps (or at least rests from time to time). Unlike their wild cousins that receive water, fertilization, and so on naturally, houseplants need our assistance to thrive. Most times when you buy a plant, it will come with a care tag that outlines its light, water, and air temperature requirements. An in-depth look at each of these aspects of plant care, and more, follows. (Note that the Go-To Plant List beginning on page 32 includes details about the featured plants' care needs.)

LIGHT

In their natural environments, some plants (like philodendrons) cling to trees and receive dappled sunlight, while others (like cacti) are out in the open and exposed to full sunshine all day. While plants are adaptable, in order for them to flourish, they should be kept in your best approximation of their preferred lighting conditions. If you set a sun-loving plant in a windowless room, it won't survive for long—but it'll likely do fine with bright light instead of direct sun.

The lighting conditions in any home are determined by many factors. If you're on the top floor of an apartment building and have an expansive view, you'll have different light than if you're on the bottom floor of the same building. Depending on where you live relative to the equator, season may matter, too: in the United States, winter days are much shorter than summer days (and the light is less intense and of a lesser quality). That

sun-hungry plant of yours might need a light boost in winter (see tip, above).

Light is difficult to precisely measure without a light meter, but there's no need to run out and get a piece of equipment. Opposite are general explanations of the common categories of lighting conditions (essentially, light's intensity drops as the distance from a window increases).

LIGHTING TIPS

- Some plants bend toward light, and others bend away from it. Rotate plants if you want them looking good from all angles (set heavy plants on a lazy Susan or on a wheeled plant stand).

- Plants can sunburn. Move them from shade into direct sunlight gradually, not in one fell swoop.

- Clean dirty windows and remove screens to allow maximum light to reach your plants.

- Help your plants cope with suboptimal lighting or short winter days by placing a lamp above them. Any bulb will help, as long as it is used in addition to *some* natural light (a regular incandescent lightbulb won't be enough for a plant in a dark corner if it is the *only* source of light). If using only artificial light, you'll need an LED bulb (see page 117 for details).

- White walls and mirrors help bounce light around a room and give plants a boost.

- Sunlight in the morning (and very late afternoon) is of lesser quality, is less intense, and is cooler than the rays in midday and early afternoon. If a plant calls for bright light but cooler temperatures, be sure to place it in a spot that avoids midday sunshine.

Direct Light

Direct light means the sun is shining right on the plant for about half the day. If you're in the northern hemisphere, like here in the United States, a south-facing window is the perfect home for plants that like direct light.

Bright Light

This is the indirect light you'd get through a sheer curtain or right next to a window that doesn't have sun shining *directly* onto the surface below it. If you hold your hand over a blank piece of paper in this spot, you should see a defined shadow. A lot of plants like this kind of light.

Moderate Light

This is the kind of light found a few feet (1 m) inside a room's walls or right along a dim, north-facing window (in the northern hemisphere). There's no exact blueprint for this value because the luminosity depends on many factors, including the size of the window, the orientation of the sun, and any structures (awnings, trees, buildings) that may hamper the sun's rays. The best rule of thumb is that this light will produce a fuzzy shadow.

Low Light

This is the lighting condition well away from a room's source of illumination (for example, the opposite side of a room with a small window). Note, however, that low light still means *some* light—you should be able to comfortably read a book where the plant is positioned. Low light is dim, not dark. (If the light is too low for a plant, it may get spindly or its green leaves will begin to yellow.)

WATERING

When it comes to watering your plant, first consider the type of plant it is and its native environment. A succulent like an echeveria (that is accustomed to unreliable rainfall will retain moisture in its leaves and require infrequent watering, whereas a tropical plant like a croton drinks up water quickly and needs ambient humidity.

Watering frequency then will depend on several additional factors: the season (winter offers shorter days and cooler temperatures, meaning less water is needed) and the climate (Florida is more humid than Colorado), as well as the pot placement (a stand-alone planting in a sunny spot requires more water than a grouping in the shade), pot material (a breathable clay pot dries out more quickly than a plastic one), and pot size (a tiny pot needs to be watered more often than a large one). Two of the same exact plants, if placed in different environments, would require different watering schedules.

As a general rule, water your plant when the first inch (2.5 cm) or so of soil is dry. Use your finger, a water gauge, or a chopstick to measure soil moisture (for the latter, a brown line will appear on the chopstick at the point where the soil is moist). Weight is also a helpful indicator—lift the pot before and after a good soaking to feel the difference between parched and drenched soil. Beyond that, watch the plant—it will likely wilt when it needs water. If the plant hasn't been without water for too long, it'll bounce right back once you give it a drink (it's cool to watch the leaves' response as they perk right up and say thank-you!). Following is a rough guide on the levels of moisture your plants may require (and remember that plants may need different levels of moisture at various times of the year).

Dry: If your plant requires dry soil, that means times of drought are okay or even beneficial. Let it dry out completely for a time before watering thoroughly. Plants benefiting from this watering method, or lack thereof, often have plump leaves, like succulents, or have adapted other clever ways to store water in their naturally drier climates.

Slightly Moist: This level of moisture works for the majority of houseplants. The key is to ensure that the top 1 inch (2.5 cm) or so of the soil dries out before you water again (for a small 4-inch/10 cm pot, it'll be the first ¼ inch/6 mm).

Evenly Moist: For plants that require evenly moist soil, don't allow the soil to dry out at all between waterings. Moist soil is comparable to a wrung-out sponge—soft, plump, and slightly wet, but not soggy.

HOW TO WATER YOUR PLANT

There are many ways to water a plant: soak it in a bowl of water, the sink, or the bathtub and let it drink from below (don't soak for longer than an hour); sprinkle water from above onto the leaves; precisely water the soil below the foliage; mist the leaves; or let it make its own "rain forest" in a cloche or a closed terrarium (see page 24). Some plants prefer certain methods, which will be indicated in the pages that follow when necessary, but when in doubt, the best option is to water the soil, not the leaves. Whatever method you choose, room-temperature water is best. Generally speaking, when it's time to water, let the water fully saturate the soil. After watering, place the vessel on a saucer, let the water run out of the bottom of the pot, and discard the excess water.

WATERING FAQS

Below are a few common questions you may have when it comes to watering your plant. If your plant just doesn't seem happy, or isn't drinking up its water like it should, consult this rundown for a few easy fixes that'll perk a thirsty plant right up.

Is the water running off instead of soaking in? If so, the soil may be compacted. Make a few holes in the soil with a chopstick or fork and water again. The plant may also be root-bound (see "The Grow Pot," page 12); in this case, it's time to repot to create more space for soil and moisture to mingle in with the roots.

Has the soil separated from the edges of the pot, or is water quickly running right through the pot and not soaking in? This is an indication that your soil has completely dried out and needs to be rehydrated. If your pot has drainage holes, hold the pot in a bowl of room-temperature water. Let go when it starts to absorb water and stops floating, then soak for an hour or so to let the soil fully absorb moisture. If your pot doesn't have drainage, fill the vessel with water, wait, and repeat until the soil is plump. Then gently tip the vessel out over a sink to drain any pooling excess water.

Think you've overwatered? Gently free the plant from the pot (it should come out with soil and roots intact). Then lightly pat down the edges of the soil using paper towels to absorb some of the excess water. Let the plant stand, unpotted, on a plate until it becomes just moist to the touch, then return it to the pot.

Going on vacation? If you'll be gone for only a week or so, a simple solution is to give your plants a good drink before you leave and cluster them together to raise humidity and slow evaporation from the soil. You can create a similar effect by placing pots on a gravel tray (see page 24) or even gently covering your plants with lightweight plastic (think dry cleaner bags) to create a temporary greenhouse effect. For a longer trip, consider purchasing a water globe, a wick-watering mechanism, or even self-watering pots. You can also make your own water-releasing contraption: Set a jug of water next to your plant. Cut pieces of natural twine into sections long enough to reach from the jug to the plant, then place one end of each piece at the bottom of the water jug and stick the other an inch into the soil surface. The standing water next to the plant will increase humidity, while the twine will replenish moisture in the soil as it dries out. Of course, you can also ask a friend or neighbor for a favor or even hire a professional plant sitter!

Use a narrow-mouthed watering can to more precisely water plants that don't like to get their leaves wet, like this Cape primrose.

HUMIDITY

A lot of plants (and humans) feel most comfortable in 60 percent relative humidity. If you have artificial heating or cooling in your home or live in an arid climate and you are growing humidity-loving tropicals, you'll probably need to increase the moisture in your air. Here are six techniques.

1. Group plants together so that they help keep one another moist.

2. Set pots on a waterproof tray filled with gravel, and add a thin layer of water (make sure the gravel keeps the pots above the waterline). As the water evaporates, it will humidify the surrounding air.

3. Cover or contain your plants under a cloche or in a terrarium.

4. Move your plants to a more humid room, like the bathroom.

5. Add a humidifier to the room.

6. Mist your plants. A spray bottle filled with water will only *slightly* improve humidity, but the act of misting is inexplicably satisfying and does clean plant leaves.

Pictured here are an African violet on a gravel tray (above) and a 'Needlepoint' English ivy in a cloche (below).

TEMPERATURE

Plants thrive with fresh air and good air circulation. A gentle, warm breeze from an open window on a lovely day is a welcome balm for most. Be mindful of blazing radiators, arctic air conditioners, and drafty winter windows, all of which create conditions too extreme for most houseplants. Be aware that your home likely has a few microclimates. When choosing where to place your plant, think about which rooms tend to be warmer or cooler than others.

Some variation in temperature is okay, however. Just like their wild cousins, houseplants can benefit from cooler evening temperatures. In cooler air, plants slow down their respiration (sugar/energy usage) and allocate energy toward maintaining their health instead of putting it all into new growth. And although plants are sensitive to temperature, they are adaptable. The recommendations below aren't strict rules—they're ideals. And of course, heat or cool your home for *your* comfort, then find plants that thrive in that kind of environment.

Chilly: Below 55°F (13°C) but above freezing. This climate is detrimental to most houseplants, but there are a few that benefit from it, including bulbs that require forcing (like hippeastrum; see page 49).

Cool: Roughly 55°F to 60°F (13°C to 16°C). For reference, this temperature may give you a slight chill, like when you enter a garage or a basement.

Average: 60°F to 75°F (16°C to 24°C). This is a wide range, and one most houseplants (and humans!) will feel fairly comfortable in.

Warm: 75°F to 80°F (24°C to 27°C). This is the climate for plants that like things toasty.

FERTILIZER

Like us, plants require nutrition. Some nutrients are obtained from the potting mix your plants are grown in, but you may want to supplement with a fertilizer during the longer days of spring and summer. The majority of houseplants will benefit from a monthly application, but some plants require a more regular regimen (twice monthly) and others will benefit from a lighter application (every two or three months). The Go-To Plant List beginning on page 32 includes information on how frequently to fertilize; it's often best to cut out fertilizer completely in the winter months (when growth tends to slow or the plant enters a dormant period and needs rest).

Fertilizer is offered in powder, liquid, and pellet form, and will be marked with three numbers that indicate the percentages of nitrogen (N), phosphorus (P), and potassium (K) in the mixture. Different combinations promote leaf growth, root growth, blooming, and fruiting, but a "general-purpose" natural fertilizer offers a solid one-stop-shopping option. When I fertilize, I like natural blends such as fish or seaweed. There's more wiggle room in terms of timing and measurements with natural by-product blends, since they generally supply lower levels of nutrients than chemical fertilizers do. If opting for a liquid fertilizer, water the soil first to increase absorption.

Regardless of the formula you choose, it pays to be conservative in your application—less is more. Overloading the soil with nutrients is often more detrimental than avoiding fertilization completely, as it can burn the plant's roots and cause distress. Especially with chemical fertilizers, I recommend skipping the manufacturer's instructions and using a half-strength mix instead.

PLANT SOS

Plants show you what they need. Caring for them is a matter of understanding and interpreting their signals and, when needed, changing things to keep them healthy. Here are some common maladies and possible solutions. If you're really in a pinch, head to the Royal Horticultural Society website (RHS.org.uk/advice) for help with plant diagnostics and suggested remedies.

Wilting or Curling Leaves: The most common cause of wilting or curling leaves is either underwatering or overwatering. If the pot feels lighter than usual, it is a good indication that the soil has dried out and needs water. Conversely, if when you lift the pot, there's a pool of water in the saucer, you've been overzealous with the watering can. Empty the saucer and soak up any sogginess in the soil with a rag or newspaper. If water doesn't seem to be the issue, consider temperature. Heat can make a plant wilt, and curling leaves can be brought about by cold drafts near windows, doors, or open hallways. Aphid bugs can also cause curling, as they suck the juices out of a plant's leaves. If you spot these soft-bodied bugs, wipe them away or blast them with a faucet's spray to remove them.

Brown or Yellow Spots on Leaves: Spots and patches on leaves are usually a sign of either a watering issue or pests. Do some investigating—brown crispy tips signal underwatering or low humidity; brown soft spots may mean you've been overwatering. It could also be a fungus or blight—remove any damaged leaves and make sure your plant has good air circulation. Speckles on the surface of the leaves or a blister-like appearance may indicate

that you have unwelcome scale insects. Remove these critters with a cotton swab soaked in rubbing alcohol, and be diligent—they're tough to conquer once they've interloped. Finally, if you've recently moved your plant from shade to a sunny spot, it may be sunburned—always move plants from shade to sun in stages to acclimate them.

Ragged or Holey Leaves: If holes or notched edges suddenly appear on the leaves of your plant, it's likely that the plant is hosting some sort of chewing insect. This can be treated fairly easily—pick off any adults and spray the affected area with soapy water. Evidence of snail activity usually includes a trail of shiny slime. Look in nooks and crannies where snails might be hiding from daylight.

Wrinkled or Shrunken Leaves: Naturally fleshy plants like succulents (including cacti and sansevieria) will let you know when they're receiving too much or too little water. Gently touch a leaf: if it's hard and wrinkled, it's time to water; if it's soft and prune-like or has gone to mush, it's a sign you may have been overwatering.

Falling Leaves: It's quite normal for leaves to fall off some new or recently repotted plants. Give those plants time to acclimate, and prevent shock by slowly and gradually moving them from an area of low light to one of bright light. If you haven't recently moved or repotted your plant, falling leaves could be due to an undesirable temperature change or could signal overwatering or underwatering (check your plant's requirements). If the leaves progress from healthy green to pale then darker yellow and finally fall off, give your plant a gentle shake—if a cloud of tiny flying bugs appears, you're dealing with a white fly infestation (for treatment options, see the box below). And remember, it's natural for leaves to fall off your plant—old leaves will sometimes fall and be replaced by new growth.

Leggy Stems: Spindly growth, also called etiolation, is a hint that your plant isn't receiving enough light and is on the prowl to find it. The flat rosettes of an echeveria are particularly susceptible to such wanderings if left without adequate light. (Other telltale signs your plant is light deprived include small leaves, pale green growth, and leaf loss.)

Sticky Stuff: Leaves that are sticky to the touch may be home to unwanted guests. The stickiness is not from the plant but is a substance called honeydew, excreted by an insect pest. There are many different pest treatments out there. Most are pest specific, so it may require a process of elimination to find the right remedy.

Guttation: This is not as horrific as it sounds! Guttation is the term for tiny water droplets forming on leaf tips. Unlike dew, which settles on the leaves, this water comes from *inside* the leaf and is caused by wet soil (when the plant takes in too much water and pressure builds, which forces moisture to be exuded as little droplets). You're most likely to notice this phenomenon in the morning before moisture has had a chance to evaporate.

Roots Abound: If roots are popping out of the pot's drainage holes, it might be time to repot. Gently lift out the plant; if it's one mass of tightly knit roots, it's time for an upgrade. If you want your plant to grow larger, slightly increase the pot size: break up the roots with your hands (or a clean knife), remove

a portion of the soil, add some fresh potting mix to the pot, and replant. If you want to keep the plant about the same size, see the box on the next page for instructions. (See page 17 for more on repotting.)

Sadly, a lot of plants are killed with kindness—often with too much water. To make the situation worse, after just one bad run, folks say, "I'm a plant killer!" Having a plant die on your watch may be disheartening, but please don't give up. Some plants are expected to live for years and years, while others, like a gerbera daisy, may make only a quick stopover. Don't be hard on yourself if a plant friend fades away—I've had plenty move on to the compost pile. It's all about practice, trial, and error. Just say, "Thank you; it was fun knowing you. I'm so glad we had this time together." Then try again!

A WORD ABOUT BUGS

The first layer of defense against pests is to keep your plant healthy. Insect troublemakers are on the lookout for an easy prospect and are more likely to infest a run-down plant than a vigorous one. If you find an insect intruder, segregate your plant (or even set it outside) until it has healed, and be consistent with your treatment. If you catch the bugs early (and they aren't flying off everywhere), start by simply washing them off with water. You'll need to rinse, wipe, and repeat for a few days after they disappear. For a stronger line of defense, try applying rubbing alcohol to the infested areas with a cotton swab, or mixing a few drops of natural dish soap with water and applying with a spray bottle or cloth. For specific treatments, you can take a photo of the infestation and bring it to a plant nursery or Cooperative Extension master gardener and ask for assistance. If things get serious, and bugs abound, consider bringing your plant to the compost bin so that those creepy crawlers don't spread to other plants.

SHAPING YOUR PLANT

Plants have their own natural forms (draping, upright, bushy), but with help from humans, they can be manipulated into all sorts of shapes. Bonsai plants, for example, are kept small, while topiaries are groomed to a particular form, and espaliered plants are trained against a wall. Stems can even be grown over structures to create curved configurations or woven into living art (see the braided spear sansevieria on page 207, for example). Here are a few simple techniques for shaping your plants.

PRUNING

We prune plants both for aesthetic reasons and for the health of the plant. You may want to keep your plant a certain size or make a straggly or spindly plant fuller and bushier by trimming to encourage branching and growth.

Plants can also be pruned into whimsical shapes like elephants or more classic topiary shapes like lollipops. The variegated dwarf umbrella plants on the opposite page, for example, have been pruned and trained differently from the start of their lives. If allowed to grow naturally, the plant on the right will continue to spread up and out in a wild bushy form. In contrast, the plant on the left has been carefully pruned, with new growth removed along the trunk, to create its tree-like shape. If a plant has a broken stem or a section ravaged by diseases or bugs, pruning will freshen it up. And once a flowering plant is done blooming, deadheading (snipping the spent blooms) will keep it from setting seed and thus may encourage it to bloom again.

When pruning, always use a clean, sharp blade. Make a quick, clean 45-degree-angle cut just above a node (where the new shoot will form).

KEEPING YOUR PLANT'S SIZE IN CHECK

Some plants, like the rubber plant, will keep on growing as you increase their pot size. If your plant's roots are popping out of the soil but you want to keep it the same size rather than transfer it to a larger pot, unpot the plant, and with a clean sharp knife or pruners, gently shave off about 1 inch (2.5 cm) around the perimeter of the root-ball. Add fresh potting mix to the same pot and replant.

Pictured here are two different variegated dwarf umbrella plants (*Schefflera arboricola* 'Variegata'), one pruned and trained (left) and the other allowed to grow wild (right).

ADDING SUPPORT

The first form of support you may encounter is a stake tied to the main stem or trunk of your plant when you purchase it from a nursery. This holds the tree or plant upright during transportation. However, the green tape and bamboo poles often used to secure plants might not be aesthetically pleasing, and the overall shape of your plant may need some adjusting. To restake your plant, first carefully snip the tape that holds the plant's stems to the stake. Move from the bottom to the top, slowly supporting each stem as you go with your hands. Gently let the stem go. Repeat with each stake. Once the stems are free, shape and support as you wish. Experiment with green twine and stakes that can be camouflaged, or go for something bright and attention grabbing.

Support structures can take many other forms, too: a hidden stake around which young plant stems are braided (as shown here, on the left), a wire hoop on which a hoya grows to create a living sculpture (see page 51), a single stick holding up a floppy-headed orchid (see page 171), a series of wall hooks supporting a vine (see pages 194 and 214), or a trellis on which you've espaliered a plant (see page 203).

Finally, pruning and adding support go hand in hand. You'll need snips and twine or twist ties handy to help guide and support your upwardly or outwardly crawling green friend.

SHARING YOUR PLANT

Sharing a plant is a meaningful endeavor. It's an easy and affordable gesture of trust, friendship, and community spirit. Plus, seeing how someone else shows off your living gift—with vase choice, placement, planting technique—is a fun way to collaborate, learn, and be inspired. Some plants that are particularly easy to propagate are featured in part I along with specific instructions (see pages 72, 84, 89, and 90). Here are a few simple ways to share your plants.

OFFSETS

Offsets are essentially baby plants that are produced from a mother plant. With plants that produce offsets, like bromeliads (see page 37) and some succulents (see page 89), simply pluck or cut, place in a pot, and share!

ROOTING

Rooting is the process by which a cutting or piece of plant is placed in water, perlite, or a potting mix until new roots form. Adding rooting hormones can help with faster and better root formation. Pelargoniums (see page 66) and pothos (see page 74) are good candidates for this method. Once roots form, the tiny plant can be planted in a potting mix.

DIVIDING

Sometimes you must dig deep into the soil to propagate plants. To divide a plant, unpot your specimen and separate the root clump. Some break apart easily, like the bulbs of the oxalis (see page 62), while others have more tenacious root systems and require a sharp knife. Once separated, replant in fresh potting mix.

Dividing plants can take some muscle, especially when the roots are tenacious (like in the case of this ZZ plant). Don't be afraid to really yank them apart or, if needed, employ a sharp knife for assistance.

CHILD AND PET SAFETY

Any poisonous plants featured in this book will be noted as toxic. In the context of this book, *toxic* does not automatically mean deadly—severity and symptoms vary. As a precaution, you may want to keep all plants out of reach of small children and animals. Some plants, like the ZZ, aren't dangerous to touch but are harmful if ingested, while others that deter predators with sharp thorns (like cacti) or irritating sap (some euphorbias) may injure your skin with the slightest touch. Visit the ASPCA website (ASPCA.org) for a list of pet-safe plants. A few common poisonous plants to look out for include chrysanthemum, gardenia, hellebore, hippeastrum, monstera, pothos, rex begonia, sago palm, sansevieria, schefflera, and pencil cacti.

PART I

THE GO-TO PLANT LIST

Why bring plants into your home? Because they are amazing. They make the world go round. We eat them, we build houses with them, we wear them and dye our clothes with them, we use them to develop fragrances and to make medicines. Gardening and caring for plants can promote mental and spiritual well-being through a practice called horticultural therapy. Plants are mighty powerful and oh so valuable.

There are so many wonderful houseplants, it would be impossible to show off every exemplary choice. The pages that follow feature some of my favorite easy-to-find, easy-to-care-for options. For each featured specimen, you'll find basic care information, including its soil, light, water, fertilizer, and air temperature requirements (see pages 14 and 20–25 for detailed explanations of these). Here, in part I, these stars take center stage; in part II, you'll find them displayed in myriad ways throughout the home. I hope that their stories springboard you into the wondrous world of playing with plants!

AIR PLANT

The perfect companion for the hands-off trendsetter

THE BASICS

CARE LEVEL
Easy

LIGHT
Moderate to bright

SOIL
Not required

WATERING
See box, below

FERTILIZER
Use every few months,
only in spring and summer

TEMPERATURE
Average

SIZE
Tabletop

Tillandsias, or air plants, are members of the bromeliad family and include more than five hundred different species of epiphytes, plants that anchor onto other plants and outcrops, absorbing rainfall and nutrients with their leaves. This unique trait has enabled them to flourish across a spectrum of environments, from dense rain forests to stark sand dunes.

Hailing from the sun-soaked tree trunks of Mexico, Guatemala, and El Salvador, *Tillandsia xerographica*, pictured here, is (as the name suggests) one of the xerophytic air plants. Efficient at soaking up limited moisture and nutrients from the air, xerophytes' trichomes (the scales and hairs on the leaves) give the plants a white or silvery flocked appearance and help reflect the harsh rays of the sun. Its leaves wrap and twist as it grows, giving it a similar appearance to *Tillandsia streptophylla* but with greener, velvety leaves sprouting from a longer stem. Drier conditions and shadier locations will cause tighter coils to form. These air plants are perfect for display on windowsills and shelves where their silver ripples can cascade. *See more air plants (including a much smaller* T. xerographica*) on pages 238–239 and 246–247.*

HOW TO WATER YOUR AIR PLANTS

There are three ways to water air plants: misting, dunking, and soaking. Choose a method that works with your schedule. You can mist daily, and supplement with a good soak occasionally. Go one step further by dunking your plant under a running tap or showerhead for a few seconds once a week. If you're often on the go, soak every ten days or so in cool tap water for up to a couple of hours. Rid plants of excess water by gently shaking them before returning them to their home. Note that naturally humid environments will call for less frequent watering.

BILLBERGIA BROMELIAD

A South American native shows off a festival of colors

THE BASICS

CARE LEVEL
Moderate

LIGHT
Moderate to bright

SOIL
Peat moss mix

WATERING
Let dry between waterings;
water less in winter;
provide humidity

FERTILIZER
Use monthly; skip in winter

TEMPERATURE
Cool to warm

SIZE
Tabletop

Bromeliads are a diverse family of tropical plants made up of more than three thousand species. They're a tribe of many forms and functions, from epiphytic specimens like air plants (see page 34) to terrestrial earth stars (see page 252). Pineapples are even a part of this gang!

Billbergia nutans, or queen's tears (pictured here), is native to Brazil, Uruguay, and Argentina and is one of the easiest to care for in the clan. It should be watered directly in the center of its rosette. Be careful when handling—the plant's long, saw-toothed leaves stack to form rosettes up to 15 inches (38 cm) high, and it can deliver a prickly bite. Its main virtue is its arching flower stalk, which explodes in a whole carnival of colors.

If this vibrant display isn't enough to entice, bromeliads have one more quality that's sure to win you over: they are prolific at producing offsets, called pups. Replant pups when they reach a third of the size of the parent plant (waiting for them to grow to this size will allow roots to develop more successfully). Remove the entire plant from its planter and, using a sharp knife, cut the pups off as close to the parent plant as possible, retaining a good hunk of roots. Replant a group of pups in a small pot filled with peat moss mix, place in a bright area, and keep the soil evenly moist. Ideally, the pup will have roots when you remove it. If it doesn't, don't panic—roots will eventually form; in the meantime, support the plant with wooden sticks. (Resist the temptation to push the pup deeper into the potting medium, as this can rot the base of the plant; 1 inch/2.5 cm or less is plenty, with support.) Move to an area of moderate light once mature. *Find other varieties of bromeliads on page 231.*

◁ This bromeliad's species name, *nutans*, is Latin for "nodding" and refers to the pendant clusters that hang from its bright pink stalks. These unroll to present royal blue petals with elongated canary-yellow stamens.

BOSTON FERN

A mutant stowaway that has stood the test of time

THE BASICS

CARE LEVEL
Easy

LIGHT
Moderate

SOIL
Potting mix

WATERING
Keep evenly moist;
provide humidity

FERTILIZER
Use monthly; skip in winter

TEMPERATURE
Average to cool

SIZE
Tabletop to floor

The best things sometimes happen by accident, and this fern is no exception. Descended from a mutation of a swordfern, the Boston fern (*Nephrolepis exaltata*, also known as the Boston swordfern) was so named because it was reportedly discovered on a ship to Boston in 1890. Thanks to its showstopping frilly green fronds (which can reach an impressive 3 feet/1 m in length), it was soon a quintessential feature of Victorian parlors; it later became a bohemian mainstay, filling macramé planters throughout the 1960s, and it continues to hang elegantly from baskets, pedestals, and pots in homes today.

This fern's fast-growing nature means you can cultivate a statement piece relatively quickly. (Opt for dwarf varieties if space is an issue; otherwise, these specimens will soon be demanding expansive real estate.) With its thirst for humidity, the Boston fern often thrives when kept in a bathroom. If it doesn't receive enough moisture, it will soon drop a full frond's worth of leaflets, so it can be a messy houseguest if neglected. But don't worry—it is durable and bounces back relatively quickly once moisture levels are restored. For ways to increase humidity, see page 24. *See more ferns on pages 222–225.*

CAPE PRIMROSE

A graceful plant with endless blooms

THE BASICS

CARE LEVEL
Moderate

LIGHT
Bright to moderate

SOIL
Peat moss mix

WATERING
Keep evenly moist to slightly dry; provide humidity

FERTILIZER
Use every few weeks, only in spring and summer

TEMPERATURE
Cool to average

SIZE
Tabletop

◁ See the green plastic rim on the inside of this ceramic vase? That's the plant's original grow pot. For an oh-so-easy plant display, simply pop your plant, grow pot and all, into a more stylish vessel for an instant upgrade. See page 15 to learn more.

Cape primroses (*Streptocarpus* hybrid) are found in wooded ravines in South Africa, where they lie lapping up dappled sunlight. With crinkled leaves and luminous floral sprays, they're a great choice for areas of your home in need of enlivening. Their year-round, trumpet-shaped flowers—in purples, pinks, whites, and lavenders—offer a cheery antidote to short winter days and a happy encouragement of long summer nights.

The deep green color of their gently curved, rather large wrinkly leaves is enhanced in low light (avoid direct light, which can scorch them). Occasionally pluck older leaves and snip faded flower stems to ensure that your primrose stays tidy throughout the year. While they're relatively easygoing, these plants have rather particular watering requirements. Avoid letting water touch the leaves, which can cause staining; instead, water below the leaf level, directly on the soil, or give a soak from below. Keep soil constantly, lightly moist in spring and summer. You can let it get less moist in winter, but it should never be completely dry. If you've got the heat on high during the winter, or you live in a hot, dry climate, add a gravel tray below your planter (see page 24) not only to give the primrose's endless blooms a stage but also to maintain much-needed humidity. To try your hand at propagating the Cape primrose, simply cut a leaf and stick it back into the pot it came from. It will root—if you don't let it dry out!

DRACAENA

A hard worker with style to spare

THE BASICS

CARE LEVEL
Easy

LIGHT
Moderate to low

SOIL
Potting mix

WATERING
Keep evenly moist; water less
in winter

FERTILIZER
Use monthly; skip in winter

TEMPERATURE
Average

SIZE
Tabletop to floor

Dracaenas (also known as false palms, corn plants, or cane trees) are incredibly versatile—smaller specimens often adorn desks and tabletops, while larger plants add a pop of light in darker corners. An all-green version ('Janet Craig') is a common find, but there are so many more interesting varieties to choose from!

All of the plants pictured opposite are the same variety, *Dracaena fragrans* 'Lemon Lime'. Wonder why one grouping has long trunks and the other is more compact? Growers in Hawaii and other warm climates use a unique propagation method to create the different heights you see here: First, they remove the top section of a mature tall dracaena, cutting just below the leaf line and taking care to include nodes (the points where leaves or buds attach to the stem), as this is where the new plant will form roots. Then they place the new cutting in a mix of soil and perlite or put it in a vase of water, making sure the water covers the nodes but remains below the leaves. Once the cutting has rooted, the growers transplant the cutting to a grow pot to let it increase in size. This creates a planting like the one on the right. After the growers have removed the crown, there remains a bare trunk arising from the soil. New shoots will eventually form from the cut edge. In the case of the three-trunked dracaena planting pictured opposite (left), the growers planted three rooted trunks (each cut off at a different height) in one pot—it looks like it was grown together, but really it was planted that way. If you're an experimental gardener, try this at home. (I suggest rooting your cutting in water, as it's rewarding to watch the roots develop.) Keep curious pets away, as this exotic plant is toxic to cats and dogs.

◁ *Dracaena fragrans* comes in many interesting colorways, from the enticing yellow and green stripes of 'Dorado' (top) to the white swirls of 'Malaika' (middle) and the refreshing stripes of 'Lemon Lime' (bottom and opposite). For a solid hit of color, choose the bright lime green of 'Limelight', as seen on page 197.

FATSHEDERA

Bring the outside in with this garden favorite

THE BASICS

CARE LEVEL
Easy

LIGHT
Low to bright

SOIL
Potting mix

WATERING
Keep evenly moist in spring and summer; let dry slightly between waterings in fall and winter

FERTILIZER
Use monthly, only in spring and summer

TEMPERATURE
Average

SIZE
Tabletop to floor

Originally discovered in 1910 tucked away in a garden in Nantes, France, fatshedera (× *Fatshedera lizei*) is something of a botanical anomaly. Whereas most hybrids are created between species in the same genus, this marvel inherited its offbeat features from cross-pollination between two genera in the Araliaceae family, the upright Japanese aralia (*Fatsia japonica*) and the sprawling vines of English ivy (*Hedera helix*), making it a bigeneric hybrid. Finding itself somewhere between a climber and a shrub, this plant (tellingly called tree ivy) has a bit of an identity crisis.

Left to its own devices, it will grow in a drunken upright fashion before slouching over. However, given some attention with a pair of sharp clippers, it soon becomes extremely compliant and can quickly be trained into elegant columns and topiary. For a bushier appearance, clip straggly branches back before new growth appears in spring. Choose your desired height and cut the stems off at a 45-degree angle. Provide the ivy with a supporting trellis and it will reward you with a courteous espalier of star-shaped leaves (see an example of this on page 203).

The ability of this plant to grow in the shade makes it a prime candidate for rooms that are otherwise devoid of plant life. Because tree ivy lacks the aerial roots of traditional ivy, you can safely use it to screen and conceal undesirable objects without running the risk of damaging your walls. Pictured here is the 'Angyo Star' fatshedera (× *Fatshedera lizei* 'Angyo Star'), a standout for its unusual creamy-edged, waxy leaves.

FICUS 'ALII'

There's a new fig in town

THE BASICS

CARE LEVEL
Easy

LIGHT
Moderate to bright

SOIL
Potting mix

WATERING
Let dry slightly between waterings; provide humidity

FERTILIZER
Use monthly; skip in winter

TEMPERATURE
Average

SIZE
Tabletop to floor

Similar to its beloved cousin *Ficus lyrata* but newer to the scene, 'Alii' ficus (*F. maclellandii* 'Alii') is sure to become a design-magazine darling, brightening rooms with its tropical flair. Known also as 'Alii' fig, saber ficus, and banana-leaf ficus, this remarkable plant doesn't exist in the wild—it is a cultivar developed in Hawaii (*Ali'i* indicates royalty in the Hawaiian language). It's a name befitting a plant that holds itself with both form and splendor.

This regal fig is available in a range of sizes, reaching up to 7 feet (2.1 m) or more indoors. Use smaller plants to decorate work areas or a large tree to make a statement in an open space. As it grows (ever so slowly), help it take on a symmetrical topiary-like form by removing lower leaves and nurturing its lollipop-esque shape by rotating the plant each week so that all sides receive an even dose of light. Keep new growth healthy by feeding the plant with fertilizer, spring through fall, at half strength. It will also begin to unveil a smooth gray bark. Multiple trunks are sometimes braided for added panache; in the case of the ficus shown opposite, a single trunk was manipulated to create a corkscrew-like form. This is achieved by twisting the young supple trunk around a form and letting it mature. When it is time to be sold, the form is removed, revealing a self-supporting spiraled trunk. Weeping branches hold rich green glossy leaves and—unlike their prodigal relation the weeping fig (*F. benjamina*)—they're a welcome addition to any room as they won't go scattering their assets around if moved or deprived of enough light. As with any true royal, 'Alii' ficus is always paparazzi-ready and instantly makes guests feel welcome.

◁ If you prefer a wilder, more natural style, pick out a bushy (non-topiaried) variety like the 'Alii' ficus shown here. Simply remove the supporting stakes and let it grow free.

HIPPEASTRUM

A bright bloomer for the holidays and beyond

THE BASICS

CARE LEVEL
Moderate

LIGHT
Moderate to bright

SOIL
Potting mix

WATERING
Keep slightly moist

FERTILIZER
Use monthly

TEMPERATURE
Varies by growth stage
(see right)

SIZE
Tabletop

◁ Before you run out and buy a vessel for your plant, see what you've got on hand. A hurricane lamp, like this one from Campo de' Fiori, makes for a striking twist on the conventional pot and shows off the beauty of the entire bulb.

Though commonly called an amaryllis, this indoor flower is actually a hybrid of hippeastrum. It bursts with color each winter and rivals the poinsettia for most-recognized holiday bloom. That said, it can actually flower well past the winter season—it all depends on when you plant it. Sold as dormant bulbs, budding stems, or flowering plants, hippeastrums and their red, pink, white, orange, and even striped blooms can brighten a dreary day in a flash.

If you buy the bulbs ready to burst with color, stage them in a decorative cachepot (see page 15) and keep them in bright to moderate light. If you choose to plant your own bulbs, plan accordingly: blooming takes, on average, six to eight weeks. For New Year's showstoppers, start planting in November. If you crave June blooms, plant your bulbs in April. Choose a weighty pot to hold the load of the bloom and bury the bulb in potting mix pointy side up, with its "neck" and "shoulders" above the soil surfaces; its sides like it cozy, just 2 inches (5 cm) from the edge of the pot. Place in a well-lit, warm spot and water sparingly until leaves appear. Once it is in flower, keep it out of direct sun and in a bit cooler temperature to prolong the blooming period, and keep the soil lightly moist.

Once the flowers fade, the bulbs need time to rejuvenate. Keep the plant watered and in a bright spot even after its blooms have faded (cut back the shriveled flower stalk to 2 inches/5 cm above the bulb). In spring, place the plant outdoors in a spot with dappled shade. When early fall rolls around, the plant will enter a dormant period for eight to ten weeks. During this time, move it to a cool place and reduce watering. Approximately two months before your desired bloom time, repeat the bulb-planting steps above. Note: The beauty of this plant is matched by its toxicity—keep bulbs away from young children and pets.

HOYA

A rambling vine with many guises

THE BASICS

CARE LEVEL
Easy

LIGHT
Bright

SOIL
Potting mix

WATERING
Keep evenly moist
(just shy of dry in winter);
provide humidity when not
in bloom

FERTILIZER
Use monthly; skip in winter

TEMPERATURE
Average to warm

SIZE
Tabletop

▷ Here, a metal hooped form guides
the twining stems of a hoya into a round
shape. To re-create the look, choose a
trellis, insert its base into the soil firmly,
and gently attach loose stems to the
form with twist ties.

These tropical vines (also known as wax plants or wax flowers) are classic houseplants and may send you on a nostalgic trip back to your childhood. Commonly spotted trailing from baskets, strewn across kitchens, or wrapped around poles, they're easy to grow and fun to style. Their thick, waxy leaves come in many shapes and sizes, from the flat almond shapes of *H. carnosa* to the creamy fringes of the 'Tricolor' hoya (*H. carnosa* 'Tricolor') or Krimson Queen hoya (Krimson Queen *H. carnosa*), pictured here, to the playful button-like leaves of *H. obovata* (seen on page 152). This plant likes things warm, so place it in an area of the home that suits its tender nature, and ensure that nighttime temperatures stay balmy.

Although the hoya's foliage is a spectacle in and of itself, its flowers are the real showstoppers. These sweet-scented constellations of star-shaped blooms are produced only when your plant matures; they are more likely to appear if you place the plant in a bright, warm spot and allow the roots to form a tight network by resisting the urge to repot. At first glance, you'll swear the delicate flowers are crafted from marzipan. Hoyas love predictability, so once buds appear, basically tiptoe around your plant—and let the faded flowers fall off naturally, leaving the spurs (they will reflower in the same spot). Look for fragrant varieties like *H. compacta* (commonly called Hindu rope), which will fill your room with outrageously sweet aromas. Beware that the hoya's leaves are toxic to animals.

Note: Hoyas can sometimes attract mealy bugs. If you spot the white woolly creatures on your plant, wipe the leaves and stems with water or dish soap. If that doesn't work, to protect your plants' friends, it's best to either root a bug-free cutting in water (see page 30) or dispose of the plant altogether.

MARIMO

A fuzzy aquatic oddity

THE BASICS

CARE LEVEL
Easy

LIGHT
Low

SOIL
Not required

WATERING
Top off and change water
frequently

FERTILIZER
None

TEMPERATURE
Average to cool

SIZE
Tabletop

Marimo (*Aegagropila linnaei*) are commonly called moss balls, but this name is misleading—these adorable specimens aren't moss at all. Rather, they are clumps of slow-growing green algae that are naturally found rolling around lake bottoms in places like Japan and Iceland. In Japanese folklore, the marimo is a symbol of love and good luck. Stories tell of two lovers forced apart who hatched a plan to run away together. Upon reaching Lake Akan, they both dove in, and it's said their spirits became marimo balls. Possessing the plant is thought to bring you closer to your heart's desire.

To add one of these charmers to your home, simply place the balls in clear vessels of water. These guys like things cool, so place them in an area away from heat sources and direct sunlight. Group containers of varying heights and shapes together for a big impact, or keep things sweet and simple with a single specimen. For a more interesting display, combine marimo balls of different sizes in the same vase or add aquatic sand or pebbles (readily available at pet stores) for another layer of color and texture. Larger rocks can also be added to your vessel, but clean them well beforehand to avoid cloudy water and bacteria growth. Top off the vessel's water level as needed with cool tap water, and change the water every two weeks (more often in warmer months) to keep things crystal clear.

Marimo are a great option for darker rooms that might not be suitable for regular plants. Place them on dimly lit bedside tables or tuck them into bookshelves and workspace alcoves. If you're having trouble finding these aquatic plants, or if your betta fish is looking for company, pet stores sell marimo as betta buddies.

◁ A marimo doesn't require much attention. Just give it a little swirl occasionally to mimic the natural motion of a marimo moving around a lake bed, keeping it round and healthy. If it becomes squashed in appearance and you prefer a round shape, remove it from the water and lightly roll it in the palm of your hand.

METALLIC PALM

Tough as cast iron

THE BASICS

CARE LEVEL
Easy

LIGHT
Low to moderate

SOIL
Potting mix

WATERING
Keep evenly moist; provide humidity

FERTILIZER
Use monthly, only in spring and summer

TEMPERATURE
Average

SIZE
Floor

The word *palm* often conjures up an image of large arching fronds swaying along a sun-drenched oceanfront, but the metallic palm (*Chamaedorea metallica*) is here to prove that even if you're constrained to small, dark, city quarters, you can still give your home a tropical flair.

The metallic palm, as the name suggests, is not only incredibly tough but also bears a metal-like sheen on its dark blue-green leaves, which it flaunts exceptionally well when the leaves are kept moist. At full maturity, it can reach up to 5 feet (1.5 m) in height. Its upright, almost stiff silhouette lends the plant a sense of formality, but its fishtail-shaped leaves soften the effect (and explain its other common name, the miniature fishtail palm). Among all the dark foliage, the palm's flowers are a special, infrequent attraction; these bright orange inflorescence with small red, orange, or purple blooms eventually turn into small, inedible black fruit.

Like the more common (but a little less snazzy) cast iron plant, the metallic palm is tolerant of low light—stand it in dim nooks or corners for an unexpected bit of green. The plant's slow-growing nature means it tends to be on the expensive side, but the benefit is that you can keep it undisturbed in the same vessel and position for years if you wish. If you buy a bushy specimen with several stems in one pot, feel free to divide it and spread the fishtail forms around your home, replant it in a linear planter as a screening hedge, or give extras away to friends (for more on dividing plants, see page 30).

MONSTERA

Bring home a bit of the jungle

THE BASICS

CARE LEVEL
Easy

LIGHT
Moderate to bright

SOIL
Potting mix

WATERING
Let dry slightly between waterings; water less in winter; provide humidity

FERTILIZER
Use monthly; skip in winter

TEMPERATURE
Average to warm

SIZE
Floor

◁ Planted in a coir-lined half-moon basket that's hung from the top of an old wooden door, this monstera has ample room to stretch its aerial roots and show off its leaves.

Naturally found in the understory of rain forests in Panama and Mexico, *Monstera deliciosa* has risen to the status of icon, its unmistakable perforated leaves stamping themselves all across the world of art and design. These large, beautiful leaves (which earned this monstera the nickname split-leaf philodendron) have adapted to life in the tropical undergrowth: their flat artist's-palette shape laps up what light there is to be found, and the pattern of ribbons and holes makes the plant wind resistant in storms.

To replicate the conditions of the rain forest at home, you'll want to offer your monstera bright light, high humidity, and warm temperatures (but in truth, it is fairly flexible in care requirements). One of the most unusual features of the monstera is that if left in an area of low light, it will start growing *toward* the darkness, a process called negative phototropism. This counterintuitive action is actually a clever ploy to find a light source: in nature, monstera has learned that by venturing toward the darkest parts of the forest floor, it will find the largest trees, which it then scrambles up to bathe in the light. (At home, save it the struggle and move the plant closer to a window!)

Indoors, a monstera can reach heights of up to 8 feet (2.5 m). Due to its natural growing habit, it will produce aerial roots and can turn into something of a sprawling mess. There are ways you can keep things neat and tidy, though. The easiest is by training angled stems to be more upright by gently tying them to stakes, boards, or poles (see page 29). If your style is more unkempt, go wild—let this sculptural plant spill from corners, hang jauntily from baskets, and captivate you and your guests alike. Note that the monstera is toxic to pets and mildly poisonous to humans.

ORCHIDS

Exotic-looking ladies with laid-back attitudes

THE BASICS

CARE LEVEL
Varies (see individual species)

LIGHT
Moderate to bright
(see individual species)

SOIL
Orchid bark

WATERING
Varies (see individual species);
provide humidity

FERTILIZER
Use at quarter strength every
few weeks; skip in winter

TEMPERATURE
Varies (see individual species)

SIZE
Tabletop

Don't let the glamorous looks of this plant group fool you: orchids aren't as demanding as you might think. They do require a care regimen that's quite different from that of your run-of-the-mill houseplant, but the vast range of species available means there's one to suit every level of expertise, from timid first-time buyers to seasoned orchid rangers. Here are four of my favorites.

1. ONCIDIUM

For fragrance plus a dazzling display, look no further than the orchids in the *Oncidium* genus. Many of the hybrids available in this group are faster growing than other orchids and flower many times. Commonly called dancing ladies, oncidiums feature graceful, arching stalks that bear swarms of fragrant flowers in shades of yellow, pink, purple, red, and white. Some hybrid varieties, such as 'Sharry Baby', not only stretch these dramatic displays up to 4 feet (1.2 m) but also perfume the air with a sweet chocolate aroma. Oncidiums do best in medium to bright light and average temperatures. Keep the bark medium to lightly moist in summer; from fall through spring, allow the bark to become almost dry between waterings.

2. PHALAENOPSIS

Orchids in the *Phalaenopsis* genus, called moth orchids, are widely available, affordable, and one of the easiest orchid types to care for, sharing many of the requirements of normal houseplants (including average temperatures). They produce long-lasting blooms in every shade of the rainbow and create stunning arrangements when clustered together in groups. A moth orchid can flower a few times a year from the same flower spike, with the main blooming season going from late winter through spring and with flowers lasting six weeks or longer. To encourage reflowering, you can also cut the flower spike just above a node, before the first flower on the stalk. Place in moderate light in summer and move to bright light in winter. Keep the orchid bark evenly moist, slightly less so in cooler months, without allowing it to dry out completely. A daily morning misting or setting the plant on a gravel tray (see page 24) can help provide desired humidity.

3

4

ORCHIDS *continued*

◁ A slim branch is used as a stylish support structure for this top-heavy paphiopedilum orchid (right). A few branches were also used to support the stalks of the oncidium orchid on page 59 (left).

3. ZYGOPETALUM

Specimens in the perfume-rich *Zygopetalum* genus can be a little trickier to find than other orchids (though I've picked up one at a grocery outlet on occasion). They are worth the effort to hunt down, however, as their intoxicating displays of purple, brown, and maroon petals produce sweet fragrances that easily fill any room. Look for their blooms in winter and early spring. Keep them under humid conditions in moderate shade and average temperatures, ensure moist but not soggy orchid bark medium, and provide good air circulation.

4. PAPHIOPEDILUM

Paphiopedilum orchids, otherwise known as lady's slippers or slipper orchids, are characterized by their big, bellowing blooms. Two side petals and a "top hat" frame the central slipper-like pouch; the flowers come in striking shades of white, green, deep purple, and yellow. Even when it's not in bloom, this orchid possesses eye-catching leaves that are sometimes mottled and can grow 6 to 12 inches (15 to 30 cm) long. Found naturally on the forest floor, these plants can tolerate moderate light. Place one in front of a mirror to view its eccentric outfit from all angles. When the orchid bark medium is almost dry, run room-temperature water through the pot until it comes out the drainage holes. Temperature preferences are cool to average. Try placing your slipper orchid in a terrarium, as it really benefits from ambient humidity.

OXALIS

A dancing shamrock

THE BASICS

CARE LEVEL
Easy

LIGHT
Moderate to bright

SOIL
Potting mix

WATERING
Keep evenly moist

FERTILIZER
Use monthly, only in spring
and summer

TEMPERATURE
Average

SIZE
Tabletop

The "nuisance" oxalis family is often scorned by gardeners for its tendency to invade spaces in the landscape. In the home, however, these specimens' ability to grow quickly is a pleasure, and their tenacity means they are long lasting and can be passed down through generations.

The signature lucky three leaves of the oxalis sit proudly atop long, sprightly stems that can reach up to 1 foot (30 cm) tall, with colorful displays of foliage like those of the Charmed Wine varietal pictured here. Delicate trumpet-shaped flowers appear in spring and summer, creating a canopy of contrast as they hang above the darker foliage below. And this dainty specimen has a secret: as the light dips and night falls, the leaves fold neatly together like a butterfly at rest, opening again as the sun rises. This slow, rhythmic cycle is called a nastic response, and it's mesmerizing and enchanting to all who observe it. (See page 198 for another sleepy specimen.)

The oxalis possesses a second superpower, too: its seeming ability to revive itself from the dead! Oxalis is grown from tiny bulbs, and each bulb acts as a safe house, allowing the plant to retreat and take refuge from extremes in temperature, lack of watering, or other environmental dangers, meaning that short periods of dryness are not devastating. Their tubers (bulbs) also make this plant easy to propagate—just divvy up the bulbs and plant. In addition to being triggered by external "dangers," this dormant period is a completely natural phenomenon and indoors can occur every few years. Should this happen to your oxalis, stop watering and resume again when new growth appears. Either way, a little care and patience will soon have it peering happily above the soil surface again. This hardy specimen has another protective mechanism—it's toxic to small pets and humans, though its strong taste deters most curious creatures before they'd ingest enough to cause harm.

PALM

A symbolic specimen for every space

THE BASICS

CARE LEVEL
Easy to moderate, depending on specimen

LIGHT
Moderate to bright, depending on specimen

SOIL
Potting mix

WATERING
Keep evenly moist; can let dry slightly between waterings; provide humidity

FERTILIZER
Use monthly, only in spring and summer

TEMPERATURE
Warm

SIZE
Tabletop to floor

Long before it became a ubiquitous symbol of tropical vistas, this ancient plant is thought to have sprouted up alongside the dinosaurs. In the millions of years since, the palm has picked up more than a few evolutionary advantages, and its 2,500 species have spread across deserts, rain forests, and myriad environments in between.

Posing as a tree, the palm is actually a flowering plant and part of the monocotyledon family. Large architectural specimens such as the kentia palm (*Howea forsteriana*) pictured here (left) require only moderate light and work best in airy rooms where they can splay out in all their tropical splendor. Mount their large pots on wheels so you can easily move them around as they grow, and rotate the pots to ensure even lighting on all sides. (If you are relocating your palm, avoid placing it in an area subject to sudden changes in temperature and lighting, which can stress it.)

Place younger and smaller versions like the areca palm (*Dypsis lutescens*) pictured here (right) on pedestals as living sculptures. When they grow taller, their foliage can be used as screens and room dividers—or try placing them next to mirrors for layers of opulence and patterns that sway around the room.

If you don't need the height but you're craving the look of a palm, go for a sago palm (*Cycas revoluta*), pictured here (center). Though not a true palm, this low, wide plant that has been around since prehistoric times offers a similar look; put one of these small-scale specimens on a desk or coffee table in bright light and watch it grow at an island-time pace (though beware that it's toxic to both humans and animals if ingested).

PELARGONIUM

The epitome of fragrant foliage

THE BASICS

CARE LEVEL
Easy

LIGHT
Direct to bright

SOIL
Potting mix

WATERING
Keep slightly moist; can let dry between waterings

FERTILIZER
Use monthly; skip in winter

TEMPERATURE
Average

SIZE
Tabletop

Pelargoniums and geraniums are members of the same Geraniaceae family, and their names are often used interchangeably. This isn't strictly correct, though: true geraniums are hardy, herbaceous plants that can survive cold winters; pelargoniums, on the other hand, are tender plants and must be brought indoors in cold temperatures. To further confuse matters, pelargoniums are sometimes referred to as scented geraniums.

Pelargoniums peaked in popularity in the 1800s, when pots boasting these plants with fanciful scented leaves were mainstays in greenhouses and crowded cottage windows. With their distinct fragrances ranging from the apple-scented *Pelargonium odoratissimum* to the nutmeg scents of *P. fragrans*, they were soon plucked from flowerpots and put to work in potpourris, food recipes, and ointments. The 'Attar of Roses' variety pictured here became an inexpensive substitute for rose oil used by the French perfume industry.

Although it's the crinkled, fragrant leaves of this plant that steal the show, edible pink flowers are produced to varying degrees in spring and summer and can be used as a lovely little garnish for sorbet.

PEPEROMIA

A half-pint houseplant with a mighty impact

THE BASICS

CARE LEVEL
Easy

LIGHT
Bright to moderate

SOIL
Potting mix

WATERING
Keep slightly moist; can let dry slightly between waterings; provide humidity

FERTILIZER
Use monthly; skip in winter

TEMPERATURE
Average to warm

SIZE
Tabletop

Grown for their ornamental foliage and compact size, members of the peperomia family are undemanding and versatile houseplants. Naturally found on the forest floor, they thrive in shady, warm, moist conditions. Paradoxically, their thick, fleshy leaves can effectively retain moisture for long periods of time, making them borderline succulents—a match made in heaven for anyone a little hands-off in their gardening approach.

The diversity of this plant genus is most noticeable in the leaves. Both cultivars pictured here have the waffle texture of their parent *Peperomia caperata* or emerald ripple peperomia. On the right is the richly colored *P. caperata* 'Red Ripple', accessorized by tail-like spikes of flowers. At left is the two-toned *P. caperata* 'Rosso'. For a marbled variety, see page 154. Hang or place these high on shelves to get the full impact of their flashy undersides.

Peperomia do best in bright or moderate light—they can tolerate low light, but they won't grow as well, and their foliage may not be as interesting. Their love of humidity and slow-growing, mounding nature make these plants a great fixture in terrariums; create a panorama of peperomia by combining colors, textures, and heights, and watch them thrive even with a bit of benign neglect. (For more ways to increase humidity, see page 24.)

PHILODENDRON

A leaf to steal your heart

THE BASICS

CARE LEVEL
Easy

LIGHT
Moderate to bright

SOIL
Potting mix

WATERING
Keep slightly moist; can let dry slightly between waterings

FERTILIZER
Use monthly; skip in winter

TEMPERATURE
Average

SIZE
Tabletop to floor

Think of this houseplant as an extension of your family, with an amicable personality and natural ability to grow in the same environment as humans. (Note: Though it coexists happily alongside humans, it is toxic—so don't get too chummy!) Although the name *philodendron* roughly translates to "tree loving," a reference to the plant's tendency to grow up trees, not all species in this group have a vine-like disposition, and even those that do need to be supported on a surface for a long time before their aerial roots attach.

The varieties that don't climb are collectively referred to as self-heading philodendrons. Characterized by dramatic and shapely leaves, self-headers form rotund clumps at their base and need a little more elbow room to grow. Soften a corner of your room with the splaying stems and undulating leaves of a Xanadu philodendron (*Philodendron* 'Winterbourn'), pictured here (left), which can reach 18 inches (45 cm) in length. With a mature plant height of 2 to 4 feet (60 to 120 cm), this variety grows into its tropical flair and looks better with age. For a classical elongated shaped philodendron, pick up the green 'Congo' variety (*P.* 'Congo'), pictured here (right). If you're looking for a playful piece with a similar leaf shape, hunt down a 'Painted Lady' philodendron, as seen on page 105. With its long, mottled, neon yellow leaves and bright pink stems, this gal knows how to work a crowd.

In general, climbing varieties grow more quickly and can tolerate lower light levels. Heartleaf philodendron (*P. scandens*) is probably the most common of the climbing bunch. Its small, heart-shaped leaves can be trained around windows, grown down poles, and left to hang off of shelves. Hanging here is a snappy 'Brasil' philodendron (*P. hederaceum* 'Brasil'), sometimes called the 'Brasil' heartleaf philodendron.

HOW TO SHARE
YOUR PILEA

When a tiny new plant emerges
from the soil and reaches about
2 inches (5 cm) tall, scoop it out
with a spoon and pop it into a
new pot of moist soil. If it hasn't
developed its own root system
(tiny hairs off the stem), place it
in enough water to cover the cut
edge of your new shoot and wait
until a few roots form.

PILEA

The designer's darling

THE BASICS

CARE LEVEL
Easy

LIGHT
Bright

SOIL
Potting mix

WATERING
Keep slightly moist; can let dry slightly between waterings

FERTILIZER
Use every few weeks, only in spring and summer

TEMPERATURE
Average

SIZE
Tabletop

Few plants have puzzled botanists as much as *Pilea peperomioides*, whose origins were so mysterious that Kew Gardens (the Royal Botanical Gardens in the United Kingdom) once put out a call in the newspaper asking readers for information on the enigmatic plant. A long and convoluted path ultimately led to the discovery of its origins in an ancient Chinese mountain range. It turns out that the plant was acquired by a Norwegian missionary living in China who brought it back to Norway in 1946. In the years that followed, he traveled widely across Europe, often bringing offshoots of this easy-to-propagate plant (see box, opposite) as gifts for family and friends. Its common name, missionary plant, honors this man, who made it possible for us all to enjoy this quirky specimen in our homes. (Its other common names, Chinese money plant and pancake plant, have to do with its leaves' unique shape.)

The versatile, easy-to-care-for specimen has recently become a collectors' favorite. Its slender stems and vivid, flat green leaves create fun silhouettes as they wave and dance, following the light. Embrace its minimalist appeal by forgoing an ornate container in favor of a plain terra-cotta or pure white vessel for a bold, clean design statement. Leave the plant in one position to create a wall of smooth green circles (as shown here), or rotate the pot two or three times a week to create a curved, parasol-like shape. Plants can reach about a foot (30 cm) tall, or larger. In some conditions, the leaves may grow as large as the palm of one's hand.

Despite their newfound popularity, pileas are harder to come by than some old standbys, and comparatively pricey as well. But their willingness to multiply with ease is a trait they share with their relative *P. involucrata*, also known as the friendship plant. If you can't get your hands on *P. peperomioides*, the crinkled leaf of *P. involucrata* is, for some collectors, much more fascinating and easier to find.

POTHOS

A "black thumb's" best friend

THE BASICS

CARE LEVEL
Easy

LIGHT
Low to bright

SOIL
Potting mix

WATERING
Keep slightly moist; can let dry slightly between waterings

FERTILIZER
Use monthly, only in spring and summer

TEMPERATURE
Average

SIZE
Tabletop

If you've struggled to keep houseplants alive in the past or if you're just getting started with plants, the pothos is almost a fail-safe. Often confused for the heartleaf philodendron (see page 70), this tropical vine is native to the isolated island chain of French Polynesia, where it tumbles down from treetops and drifts across forest floors. The coloration in the waxy leaves of the pothos is what distinguishes it from the philodendron: pothos leaves are laden with gold, white, and yellow marks (they also tend to be larger in size).

Pothos grows incredibly well indoors (reaching up to 8 feet/2.5 m long!) and is extremely versatile, though toxic to pets. Trail long vines from hanging planters or allow them to traverse across shelves and mantels. Varieties such as golden pothos (*Epipremnum aureum*) are easily found and among the simplest to grow. For an added pop of interest, choose a variegated species such as *E. aureum* 'N'Joy', pictured here (ensure that it retains its colorful foliage by placing it in an area of adequate light).

Gentle pruning once or twice a year will prevent the vine from getting too leggy. Clip vines back to as short as 2 inches (5 cm) above the soil. As a bonus, you will end up with a handful of new plants! Pothos are extremely easy to propagate and a good starting point for people with no experience. Simply take a section of vine that includes at least one leaf and a node (the point where a leaf or bud attaches to the stem) and stick the clipping in soil or a jar of water until roots form. Share with a friend or cheat your way to a voluminous look by wedging the plantling into the same pot as your original plant.

HOW TO "BASKET" YOUR POTHOS

For a fuller-looking pothos, try "basketing" its vines. Untangle its limbs, separate each vine, then one by one wind the vines around the base of your plant on top of the soil. Gently poke the vines into the soil and secure with a U-shaped piece of wire every few inches to encourage rooting.

PRAYER PLANT

A dreamy moonchild

THE BASICS

CARE LEVEL
Moderate

LIGHT
Moderate

SOIL
Potting mix

WATERING
Keep evenly moist; provide humidity

FERTILIZER
Use monthly; skip in winter

TEMPERATURE
Average

SIZE
Tabletop

Though the common name prayer plant in this book refers only to the maranta plant, both the maranta and calathea plants fall into the Marantaceae family and are often mistaken for one another. Named after sixteenth-century Italian botanist and physician Bartolomeo Maranta, both have artfully painted leaves and similar care requirements. Within the *Maranta leuconeura* species, you'll find the lemon-lime 'Marisela' variety pictured here and the more common red-veined specimen.

Prayer plants are so named for the plant's daily ceremony: listen carefully in the early dawn and dusk hours, and you may just hear the gentle rustle as it lowers and lifts its striking herringbone-patterned leaves in a nyctinastic bow to light. Some leaves may naturally brown as the plant grows—keep things tidy by occasionally pruning them.

Native to tropical Central and South America, prayer plants are low growers, taking root as their nodes creep slowly across the soil. This sprawling manner makes them versatile houseplants, allowing them to glide over tables, span interiors, and flow from hanging planters. They can grow up to 3 feet (1 m) long—if unruly stems are not your thing, trim just below a node (the points where leaves or buds attach to the stem). You can use these trimmings to propagate new plants: simply place the cutting in water until it forms new roots, then transfer to a pot with potting mix. The prayer plant is considered slightly more demanding than most houseplants, requiring relatively high humidity—turn to page 24 for tips on how to achieve this.

REX BEGONIA

It's all about that leaf

THE BASICS

CARE LEVEL
Moderate

LIGHT
Bright

SOIL
Potting mix

WATERING
Water lightly but frequently; provide humidity

FERTILIZER
Use monthly, only in spring and summer

TEMPERATURE
Average

SIZE
Tabletop

Rex begonias (*Begonia* Rex Cultorum Group) make heads turn with their dramatic leaves, which can be streaked, splashed, and swirled with an artist's palette of purples, reds, greens, pinks, and metallics. Rex begonia varieties include aptly named cultivars like the almost hypnotic spiraling leaves of 'Escargot', the exploding silver-and-plum tones of 'Fireworks', and the iridescent and cranberry double twirl of 'China Curl'. The one pictured here is 'Fairy', but they are often unlabeled—just pick the one that speaks to you!

This vibrant mass of texture, pattern, and color erupts from a thick horizontal root stem called the rhizome. It sits just below the soil and sprouts shoots and roots from its nodes (the points where leaves or buds attach to the stem). Because the rhizome lies close to the surface, rex begonias are susceptible to overwatering. If you're willing, let the leaves flag slightly before watering—but try to attend to them just before they begin to droop. Above the soil, however, it's a different story: rex begonias have a fervency for moderate to high humidity. Display alongside other plants for a showstopping centerpiece (for more ways to increase humidity, see page 24).

If the fancy-leaved rex begonia doesn't charm you, look for other varieties in this expansive genus: tuberous begonias are renowned for their blowsy blooms (see page 113); 'Sharon' begonias have eye-catching, wing-shaped leaves; and wax begonias feature waxy leaves and elegant flowers.

RHIPSALIS

A quirky cactus from the tropics

THE BASICS

CARE LEVEL
Easy

LIGHT
Moderate

SOIL
Cactus mix

WATERING
Keep evenly moist;
can let dry slightly between
waterings; provide humidity

FERTILIZER
Use monthly; skip in winter

TEMPERATURE
Average

SIZE
Tabletop

◁ That touch of bronze on the middle section of this plant tells us it got a lot of sun, and possibly too little water. Some people intentionally keep their plants in this state because they like the way it looks, but with reduced light and increased watering, the plant can bounce back from this "stress" and return to its all-green visage.

Found clinging to trees in tropical and subtropical forests, this cactus (also known as the forest or jungle cactus) is an epiphyte—hanging in shady branches and nestled between nooks and crotches of a tree (where decomposed organic matter collects), and even on rocks, rather than growing from the ground's soil, it decorates the surrounding air with its bright green and sometimes hairy stems. There are many varieties of rhipsalis, each with its own "hairstyle" and interesting quirks, from the bronzed tips of *Rhipsalis ewaldiana* to the glistening white berries of *R. baccifera* (a feature from which its other common name, mistletoe cactus, is perhaps derived). Pictured here is *R. sulcata*. For a fuzzy-tipped variety, called a hairy-fruited wickerwork cactus, see page 258 (it's the leftmost plant in the planter at the right side of the tabletop). Place your rhipsalis in a hanging planter to not only mimic its natural treetop environment but also allow you to take in the architectural configuration of its contoured green antennae.

Though rhipsalis is a cactus and requires good drainage, it does benefit from some humidity. Its epiphytic nature means you can also treat it similarly to an orchid, mounting it to a piece of wood for a vertical display (see page 234). Usually sold as a potted plant, it can survive with a small root space; wrap the root-ball in sheet moss (as you would a kokedama; see page 18) or burlap before attaching to the wood. Once your jungle cactus is mounted, water it when the soil at the base of its stems feels dry. Look out for puckering stems—this means the plant needs more water. Submerge the whole plaque in a sink or bowl of water until the soil feels moist again.

RUBBER PLANT

A polished addition to any space

THE BASICS

CARE LEVEL
Easy

LIGHT
Bright to moderate

SOIL
Potting mix

WATERING
Keep evenly moist; let dry slightly in cooler months; provide humidity

FERTILIZER
Use monthly; skip in winter

TEMPERATURE
Average

SIZE
Tabletop to floor

A valued member of the ficus genus, the rubber plant (*Ficus elastica*) is flexible in both nature and design. Gaining its common name from its sticky sap, which dries to create a low-grade rubber, it can be kept small enough to grace a coffee table or grown as a stately tree.

Outdoors, this plant can reach towering heights of up to 40 feet (12 m), and in its native habitat of India, it is used to create ornate "root bridges" (solid walkable surfaces). Grown indoors, it is less of a spectacle but equally impressive: its shiny, leathery leaves span up to 8 inches (20 cm), and the plant can reach up to 12 feet (3.7 m) tall. For a touch of opulence, go for the sumptuous darker tones of *F. elastica* 'Burgundy' (pictured here, right), or delve into the variegated creamy pastures of *F. elastica* 'Ruby Red' (left) for a playful display.

If you want a plant that's the right size for a coffee table or desk, keep your tree root-bound by restricting its growth in a small container. To create a compact, plush style, prune your plant from the top; this will cause it to branch outward, and you can control unruly side branches by trimming them off. (For more on shaping your plant, see page 28.)

Although they have a sturdy facade, rubber plants are sensitive to change, so avoid moving them around frequently or placing them in areas of extreme temperature fluctuations. They do better with high humidity, but resist the temptation to mist rubber plants, as residual water on the leaves can lead to fungal spot disease. Instead, try grouping plants together or invest in a home humidifier. Polish its leaves with a damp cloth regularly to keep them shiny. Note that the rubber plant is toxic to pets, and its sap can be an irritant to people.

HOW TO SHARE YOUR SANSEVIERIA

Divide and conquer—tease new shoots apart from the parent plant. There should be natural sections that break away easily. If your plant resists division, use a sharp knife to divide into sections—just ensure that each clump has some roots attached. Replant each clump in a new pot with fresh potting mix, and water before placing it in its new home.

SANSEVIERIA

Malleable, multicolored, and mythical

THE BASICS

CARE LEVEL
Easy

LIGHT
Direct to low

SOIL
Potting mix

WATERING
Keep slightly moist; can let dry
slightly between waterings

FERTILIZER
Use monthly; skip in winter

TEMPERATURE
Average

SIZE
Tabletop to floor

Conjuring up images of fantastical creatures and medieval weaponry, the sansevieria (*Sansevieria trifasciata*) has strong ties to enchantment and superstition. Its toxic nature and sharp, sword-like blades explain its well-deserved aliases of snake plant and mother-in-law's tongue. Sansevieria is revered in African rituals for its ability to remove the evil eye, resolve conflict, and squash tension. In China, it's treasured for bestowing the eight virtues of the gods and is thought to bring luck to anyone growing it.

In the home, this carefree and common houseplant is favored for its tolerance for neglect. It is a succulent, and its leaves store water in case of unfavorable drought conditions, making it a great choice for beginners or those who want the pleasantries of plants without a lot of upkeep. The dense growth and tall stance (reaching 4 feet/1.2 m indoors) of some varieties of this plant make it ideal for screening (see page 195): place it in front of a window or an unattractive electrical panel to provide a clever disguise (because its elongated leaves can grow quite heavy, plant in weighted, low pots to avoid toppling). Others, like the dwarf 'Hahnii' sansevieria, are really good for small containers. As a bonus, the snake plant (specifically *S. trifasciata* 'Laurentii') is considered one of the best air-purifying plants (see more air-cleaning specimens on page 188). Simply dust occasionally with a damp cloth to restore the leaves' sheen.

Pictured here is the mottled *S. kirkii* var. *pulchra* 'Coppertone'. Its stiff, slightly curved structure almost seems forged by a blacksmith, and its raw, industrial look pairs particularly well with concrete pots and brick walls. *For a more well known shape and color of sansevieria, commonly called the snake plant, see pages 188, 193 and 195–and turn to page 207 for a twisted, braided spear sansevieria.*

SPIDER PLANT

A thrilling spiller

THE BASICS

CARE LEVEL
Easy

LIGHT
Bright to low

SOIL
Potting mix

WATERING
Keep slightly moist; can let dry slightly between waterings

FERTILIZER
Use monthly, only in spring and summer

TEMPERATURE
Average

SIZE
Tabletop

The easygoing nature of the spider plant (*Chlorophytum comosum*) landed it comfortably in the free-spirited movement of the 1970s, when it first rose to popularity cascading from macramé hangers and waving its verdant ribbons of foliage. Fast-forward a few decades and it's still a staple in the home due to both its unique looks and the fact that it's one of the most tolerant houseplants around.

Introducing a spider plant to your space is a great way to bring movement and playfulness to a room thanks to the plant's fountain-like stature, with shoots spraying up from a central crown and showering down as unruly arching limbs. In addition to offering good looks, spider plants are among the top air-purifying plants for the home (for more air-cleaning options, see page 188).

Pictured here is the classic cream-and-green-striped variegated spider plant (*C. comosum* 'Variegatum'). If you're looking for something with a bit more kick, go with the swirling leaves of the 'Bonnie' curly spider plant (*C. comosum* 'Bonnie'), as seen on page 257. Whatever specimen you choose, place it in an area with abundant empty space (a shelving unit works perfectly) to allow it to stretch and show off its bountiful assets. In spring and summer, small white flowers called runners will emerge from the tips of upright wiry stems and turn into baby spider plants or "spiderettes" (see photo, left). Keeping your plant slightly root-bound by restricting its root growth in a small pot can encourage blooming.

◁ Once spiderettes form off the stems (as shown here), you can multiply your spider plant by leaving the spiderettes attached to the mother plant but placing the new growth in their own pots of soil with their nodes and roots touching the surface. Soon they'll root, and you can either cut them free to share with friends or leave them attached to create a quirky web of growth jumping from pot to pot. You can also place the spiderettes back in the same pot as the mother plant to create a bountiful, overflowing feature.

SUCCULENTS

Set it and forget it

THE BASICS

CARE LEVEL
Easy

LIGHT
Varies (see individual species)

SOIL
Cactus mix

WATERING
Allow to dry before watering

FERTILIZER
Use at half strength every few months, only in spring

TEMPERATURE
Average to warm

SIZE
Tabletop to floor

HOW TO SHARE YOUR SUCCULENTS

Succulents, particularly echeveria, can be easily propagated since they form "pups" next to the mother plant. Simply cut off any pups and set them aside for a few days until the raw ends have calloused over. Plant the stem or set the rosette in or on well-draining soil in moderate to bright light and allow to root.

The succulent group is composed of an astronomically large collection of moisture-storing plants native to almost every part of the globe and appearing in myriad colors, shapes, and textures. Given the right conditions, succulents are some of the easiest plants to care for in the home (less water is more!) and can produce spectacular displays of color year-round. Here are a few of my favorites. For more succulents to consider, see page 163.

1. KALANCHOE

From sprawling stems to fuzzy foliage, delicate flowers to contorted leaves, kalanchoe offer up a little of everything. Choose the paddle plant (*Kalanchoe luciae*), pictured, for a bold display on a small scale, or make an impact with the large, furry, fang-like leaves of Napoleon's hat (*K. beharensis*), seen on page 144. These guys like things sunny: keep in direct light in winter and bright light in summer.

2. PENCIL CACTUS

For a cleaner structure and added height go with a pencil cactus, sometimes referred to as a milk bush. The name "pencil cactus" is actually a misnomer—it's not really a cactus but a euphorbia. Handle with care, though: they produce a white sap that can be toxic to humans and pets. Pictured is *Euphorbia tirucalli* 'Sticks on Fire', whose red tips change intensity with temperature and sun exposure (they do best in direct light).

3. ECHEVERIA

The tight rosette leaves of echeveria are often what spring to mind when people think of succulents. With a wide array of colors and textures, echeveria provide containerfuls of mosaic texture. You'll need a spot with at least three to four hours of direct to bright light a day to keep most specimens compact and healthy. (If the flat rosettes begin to elongate their "necks," they're reaching out for more light.) Pictured are the neat lavender-blush leaves of *Echeveria* 'Lola'.

ZZ PLANT

Aka the "easy ZZ"

THE BASICS

CARE LEVEL
Easy

LIGHT
Low to moderate

SOIL
Potting mix

WATERING
Keep slightly moist; can let dry slightly between waterings

FERTILIZER
Use monthly; skip in winter

TEMPERATURE
Average

SIZE
Tabletop to floor

The ZZ, aka Zanzibar gem, *Zamioculcas zamiifolia*, is a tenacious houseplant. It offers a great way to dip your toes into the world of plants, especially for frequent travelers—its roots contain small reservoirs that feed the plant when it needs water. ZZs are also good for air purification (see more air-cleaning specimens on page 188), but note that they are toxic to humans and animals.

Because they are often found in dense, clumping masses of glossy foliage, it's hard to appreciate the arching symmetry of each ZZ stem. Look for less-dense specimens like the one pictured; if you can't find one, these plants are prime candidates for dividing and sharing (see box, below).

Keep the leaves shiny and healthy by wiping dust off every couple of weeks using a damp cloth. This will help them absorb the most benefits of any available light source. Although ZZs can accommodate a broad spectrum of light conditions, avoid direct sunlight (but don't leave the poor guy in the dark—even tough plants like these need *some* light to survive). The only skill one needs to care for this plant is patience: it is incredibly slow growing (which is why a floor-size specimen may be on the pricier side).

HOW TO SHARE YOUR ZZ PLANT

You'll need to be gung ho in your approach in dividing these plants—the denseness of the root-ball and tightness of the rhizomes require strategic division paths and sometimes even a pruning saw to convince the plant it wants to separate. Once you've manipulated the plant into desired sections, repot each in its own planter filled with potting mix and water. (See page 30 for an example of a divided ZZ.)

PART II

A ROOM-BY-ROOM GUIDE

Once you've picked out a plant and learned its care requirements, it's time for the fun part: figuring out how to style it and where to put it! Whether you have an expansive house or a tiny studio apartment, there is always space for a little bit of green. In the pages that follow, I'll take you through the home, suggesting plants that are particularly well suited to each location and offering myriad design solutions for spaces big and small, dim and brightly lit. My favorite go-to houseplants from part I will appear in various guises, and you'll be introduced to rarer finds as well. And after reviewing the plant design primer beginning on the next page, you will feel empowered to customize each look with whatever plant or vessel appeals to you! Read on to learn how to elevate your interior space and use the power of plants to make your house a home.

A PLANT DESIGN PRIMER

Decorating your home with plants ought to be fun and satisfying, not intimidating. The only "rules" you need to follow are the care guidelines of your chosen plant (see pages 20–25). Other than that, experiment until you find a look that's right for you! The information that follows offers some tips and tricks to help get you started.

PLANT ATTRIBUTES

Every plant you bring home has a personality all its own. The first step in deciding how best to style it in your space is to take some time to really look it over and get to know it. Here are a few important features to consider.

SIZE

Though houseplants come in a wide range of sizes, from teeny-tiny succulents to towering palms, for the purposes of this book, I describe plants as either floor plants or tabletop plants. Floor plants are your statement makers. These bold specimens can single-handedly change the feel of a room. (For more on floor plants, see page 122.) A tabletop plant, on the other hand, is just the thing for smaller spaces or to use as an accent piece or part of a more layered look.

FORM

Plants comprise many layers of shapes and structures. Each form communicates a certain feeling and mood. A tall, structural snake plant signals strength (think of an exclamation point), while a mounding 'Ming Thing' cactus evokes the softness of rolling hills. (For more on plant forms, see page 255.) Things get even more interesting when multiple forms are combined. An asparagus fern will soften that tall snake plant, adding a sense of playfulness as it dances up its column.

COLOR

When you envision a plant, you might conjure up just one shade: green. But plants are a colorful bunch! From silver to copper, canary yellow to sunset pink, plants come in colors across the spectrum, and even those that are all green tend to boast numerous verdant tones within.

TEXTURE & PATTERN

Furry, glossy, polka-dotted, or rippled. Your plant's textures and patterns are the features light will bounce off and the elements bound to turn heads. Humans are tactile creatures, after all. Think about all aspects of your plant—both sides of the leaves, and even its bark and trunk—and make sure you position it to show off your plant's full outfit (see more on placement on page 98).

VESSELS

In the pages that follow, you'll see many types of vessels, from classic terra-cotta pots to hip leather cachepots to repurposed canning jars turned terrariums. Traditional pots and vases made for planting are often the easiest options to find, and usually have predrilled drainage holes. But don't be constrained by the notion that plants belong in these common containers. Look around the house—almost any vessel (or bag, or box) can be turned into a cachepot to conceal a plant's original plastic grow pot.

Your goal is to pair plant and vessel in such a way that they will play off each other, elevating the whole look. Beyond the vessel's size (which should be as large as or slightly wider and taller than the grow pot your plant came in), here are a few factors to consider. (To learn the basics of repotting your plant or staging it in a cachepot, turn to page 15.)

COLOR & MATERIAL

The right color container can make your houseplant sing, while another hue will make it look subdued. For example, a pink earth star will pop if you place it in a contrasting white vase (see page 252), whereas its color would recede against a complementary pink one. And while the patterned leaves of a brightly colored croton plant would be highlighted by a simple, monochromatic planter (also on page 252), you can add a bit of whimsy and character to the scene by potting the croton in a vessel with its *own* wild pattern—just be sure to counterbalance this busyness by grounding the display with some neutral accessories or additional plants in solid-colored pots.

Equally impactful is the material your planter is made out of. The soft knitted plant cozy on page 120, for example, oozes comfort and softens a plant's edges. Conversely, the concrete vessel on that same page adds a tough, industrial edge to the ZZ plant's look. And the matte clay of a standard terra-cotta pot make the leaves of almost any plant radiate.

SHAPE

The shape of vessel you choose will depend on two factors: the architecture of the plant, and its intended placement in your house. The classic flowerpot shape (where the opening tapers down to a narrower base) is like the little black dress for plants: it makes almost any variety look good. A pot that is the same width from the opening to the base may make some plants look stocky or bottom heavy—use this shape only if your chosen greenery is tall or wide enough to balance it out. An hourglass-shape or pedestaled vase works particularly well for a draping specimen.

If you're using a plant as a dining table centerpiece, you'll want to stick to a low-profile bowl to ensure that your planting won't impede conversation. Conversely, a narrow hallway might call for a tall, narrow vessel. Shape also communicates a mood—a square vessel telegraphs stability and firmness, while a round one will feel approachable and warm.

STYLE

Finally, consider not only the plant's personality but also yours. If your home has a natural, rustic feel, you might want to stick your fern in a log vase, but if you're flashier, opt for a neon bowl. Whatever vessel speaks to you is a fabulous choice!

ONE PLANT, TWO WAYS

To highlight how impactful your choice of vessel can be, below I've staged one chenille plant in two different vessels (see page 15 for more on staging). As discussed on the facing page, color, material, shape, and style all impact the overall appearance of a plant-vessel pairing. Here, I've focused on the power of shape, keeping the color and texture of both vases neutral. Just adjusting this one element makes a big difference!

The Height of Elegance

A tall vase is a fitting match for any plants that drape. After a riser and a pot liner were placed in this terra-cotta pot's cavity, in went the plant in its original grow pot. The vase's curved outline adds grace and femininity to the look, and its height emphasizes the dangling flowering stems as they delicately spill out of the vessel. The warm, natural tones of the terra-cotta lend the pairing a classic, garden-like feel.

A Just-So Sprawl

The clean white veneer and widemouthed opening of this salad bowl make the unexpected vessel a pleasingly minimalistic partner for this funky chenille plant. The lush vine-like stems gently drape over the bowl's edge, just grazing the surface below, resulting in a naturalistic composition. (Be careful when pairing draping plants with low planters: if this bowl's edges were much lower, the stems could have ended up looking floppy and lifeless.)

DESIGN BASICS

The pages that follow are filled with ideas and tips to get you in the groove when it comes to designing with plants, but below is an overview of a few key concepts.

SCALE

To determine if your plant is properly to scale, you need to consider it in relation to three things:

1. **Its vessel.** As a general guideline, planters should be roughly one-third the height and/or width of your plant. For a more "Zen" design, try the opposite balance.

2. **The furniture around it.** A chunky, lived-in armchair will be able to stand up to denser planting better than a minimal bench seat. A big TV calls for an equally large plant or grouping of plants.

3. **The rest of the room.** Is the plant touching the ceiling or getting cramped in a corner? If so, it might be too big for the space. Conversely, is it too small and getting lost among the large statement pieces in the room? Maybe it needs a new home, or a few more plant friends to surround it and lend it visual mass.

BALANCE

Balance is the key to a pleasing design. In a basic sense, balance is the even distribution of weight. When you're talking about this in terms of home design, the "weight" you are looking to distribute is the visual interest in the space. Generally

speaking, you can do this one of two ways: by creating a *symmetrical* arrangement or by creating an *asymmetrical* one. Symmetry is easier to achieve—think of a matching pair of plants on either side of a fireplace—but asymmetry offers more flexibility to play with your design. See pages 124–127 for two living rooms that deconstruct these approaches.

PLACEMENT

There are many places to display your plant, whether hung from the ceiling, set on a pedestal, or resting on a shelf. The shape of both your plant and its vessel will determine much here: if it is a draping plant, let it drape—hang it or set it atop a pedestal; if it's a climber, give it something to climb. Scale also plays a role. A huge pot set on a narrow shelf would look like a boulder waiting to fall on your head. Conversely, a tiny pot on the floor may look like it has been abandoned! And think about how you'll interact with your plant, the amount of time you'll be spending around it, and the distance you'll be from it. You'll be able to enjoy far more detail on a plant that shares your desk space than on one you walk by in the hallway.

VANTAGE POINT

Consider the view you'll be gaining when situating your plant, too. Some plants are best seen from directly above—place these at lower heights to get the most bang for your buck. Others flaunt their stuff when viewed from below, so put these high up on shelves to enjoy their full potential.

Low windowsills are a great spot to highlight tiny plants with dazzling patterns or shapes, like this collection featuring (from top to bottom) a haworthia, ivy, spear sansevieria, 'Red Ripple' peperomia, and ZZ plant.

ENTRYWAY

The entryway provides a buffer between the outside world and your living space. You step in and take a deep breath, and a switch is flipped—you know you're home. With a little time and effort, you can use plants to create a smooth and pleasant transition from outdoors to in. You'll find solutions here for any kind of space, from a crowded hallway that needs to accommodate a bustling family to a grand foyer aimed at impressing guests. Strategically placed greenery can direct visitors' views or pique their curiosity by partially screening what's around the corner. Well-chosen fragrant and colorful plants in particular can also be used to set a tone. Whatever sort of space you have and whichever plants you choose, the most important thing is to let your personality shine—all the better to signal "I'm home."

FRAGRANT PLANTS

Establish your home's signature scent by placing an aromatic plant in the entry. Scent can cause many changes in the body and have an effect on mood; choose a plant to soothe (lavender) or energize (calamondin orange). If you're searching for fragrant plants, look at their botanical names—if they contain the word *fragrans* or *odoratissimum* (or any derivative of these), give 'em a sniff! Here are a few aromatic options worth bringing home.

Paperwhite

These bulbs (*Narcissus papyraceus*) make a delicate, if fleeting, addition to an entry in late fall or early winter. The strong, decidedly floral (even perfume-like) scent of their blooms may calm nerves and help relieve stress. Kept in bright light, they can bloom in either soil or water (be sure to set the top 1 inch/2.5 cm or so of each bulb above the liquid). To keep the stems short and perky when growing in water, use a mixture of one part vodka to seven parts water.

Miniature Rose

This miniature rose (a *Rosa* hybrid) is grown for the houseplant industry and adds a temporary ruffle of color to the winter home. Red blooms symbolize love; pink ones represent happiness. Place it in an area with very bright light and water regularly (but avoid getting water on the leaves). Prolong blooming by deadheading flowers as soon as they begin to fade. Rose plants will last only so long indoors, so transplant to a sunny outdoor space in spring.

THREE WAYS TO SOAK IN THE AROMA

1. **Warm the room.** Plant oils evaporate more easily and scent a space better in warm temperatures.

2. **Rub the leaves.** This works well with scented pelargoniums, eucalyptus, and herbs like lavender—give a leaf or blossom a squeeze to release the oil, and the scent will linger like perfume on your hand.

3. **Enjoy the night.** Plants emit fragrance to deter herbivores or attract pollinators. If your specimen's pollinator is active at night (like a moth), the plant will pump up its fragrance cocktail in the evening to shout, "Come and get me!" Brugmansia and some wax plants (like a cinnamon-scented hoya) are two night owls to check out.

Jasmine

Bring this sprawling vine (*Jasminum polyanthum*) inside to add its richly sweet aroma—commonly used in teas and perfumes—to your space. Its strong scent is said to improve one's mood with a single whiff. Studies have shown that its fragrance can even calm your pet. Jasmine is best kept moist and in bright light, but it is a fairly forgiving plant and can handle some direct sun as well as some shade. Tuck it in next to a broad-leaved plant for added texture.

Gardenia

Easy-to-find gardenias (*Gardenia jasminoides*) can be purchased from florists, grocery outlets, or plant nurseries and are available planted or cut. If choosing a planted specimen, get one with ripe buds to enjoy the fragrance for as long as possible. Place it in an area with bright light, and keep humidity levels high by setting the potted plant in a gravel tray (see page 24). Avoid touching any flowers, as this can bruise and discolor them.

A HARDWORKING ENTRY

The entryway is a hub of activity—boots get kicked off, coats dropped, groceries set down, and homework forgotten. But there's always room for plants! The key for bustling entries is to keep plants out of the way, whether in a basket hung securely on the wall, on a shelf, or in a custom wall unit. This will make it less likely that people will topple the plants in the whirlwind of getting out the door. Plus, hanging plants at eye level turns them into a full-on display.

The system shown opposite, created with a combination of wall-mounted pieces found at Pottery Barn, has a cohesive overall look thanks to a unifying color palette of blues, browns, and pinks that runs through the plants, vases, and accessories. Though the overall effect is one of tidiness and order, the oversize philodendron and the moth orchid (whose stem extends beyond the backdrop of the brown shelf) bring a natural softness to the look. The China doll plant (to the right of the moth orchid) is rather plain, but it pops off the shelf thanks to its white vessel with a jewel-toned green pattern. The leather wall pocket piece was sold as a garden-shed organization tool, but it works nicely as a mail sorter and air plant holder. Bonus: the *Tillandsia caliginosa* air plant (bottom right pocket) is wonderfully fragrant when in bloom.

Pretty in Pink: Did you guess that this petite pink plant is a poinsettia? Poinsettias are euphorbias and come in many shapes, colors, and sizes—see page 253 for another type. This one was placed in a felt basket (by Swedish company Aveva) lined with a coating to create a waterproof, nonbreakable vase.

Many philodendrons, like this large-leafed 'Painted Lady', are great climbers. If you're open to letting your plants grow up the wall (and potentially stick to the paint job), let them go wild!

A TABLETOP GARDEN

Bring the outdoors in with a bountiful collection of plants, unified by classic terra-cotta pots in a range of finishes. The addition of a willow trellis takes the garden theme to another level. If you need to make room for mail, keys, or other entryway ephemera, simply reduce the number of plants until you have the required space. To create your own green oasis, follow these guidelines.

Unify the grouping with matching vessels. What makes this look like an intentional design rather than a mishmash of plants is the repetition of both color and material in the vessels. Though some of the pots have a reddish hue while others are grayish, they all read as "terra-cotta" and can be effectively mixed and matched. Terra-cotta containers range from easy-to-find inexpensive versions from home and hardware stores to handcrafted, more ornate pieces found at gift shops and boutique plant nurseries.

Play with pattern and form. Though all the plants on this table are green, their varied patterns and forms make for interesting combinations. The repetition of the patterned leaves of the prayer and peacock plants (front center and far left) draws you in—making you want to get closer as their details come into view. The undulating leaf of the curly bird's nest fern (far right) is a perfect counterpoint to the upright dracaena (left)—which in turn echoes the upright, wide leaf of the snake plant (back center). The shape of the willow trellis also mimics the sweeping stems of the round-leaf calathea (front right) and the vertical stripes of its pot.

Consider scale. This huge table calls for hefty plants to balance its size, dark color, and heavy material. A grouping of small plants on this surface would look dwarfed. The tall trellis adds needed height (the asparagus fern will attach and grow on it), as does the plant stand used to raise the snake plant. Similarly, the saucer under the curly bird's nest fern (far right) is not only helpful for waterproofing but also adds a bit of bulk to balance the narrow vase.

Layer the landscape. Create an appealing, rounded silhouette by placing your tallest plants at the center, then filling in the collection with progressively shorter specimens as you near the edges of the table. An added benefit: grouped together, plants create a more humid microclimate than when standing alone, which helps them thrive.

Protect your surfaces. Waterproofing on a pristine wood table like this is a must. Either set each pot on a barrier (stand, tray, saucer, or cork coaster) and/or leave the plants in their original plastic grow pots and stage them inside decorative vessels with a plastic liner (see page 15 for more on this technique).

Against an otherwise bare wall, a blooming 'Sharry Baby' oncidium orchid adds height, while the curved vine of a Madagascar jasmine to its right creates a sense of movement.

Rise and Shine: Another solution for adding greenery in a small, busy space is a narrow plant stand like this one, which raises the plant to eye level and keeps draping flowers and leaves from touching the ground. Here a blooming cymbidium orchid adds a pop of color to lead the eye to the front door and softens the edge of the doorframe.

A FUNCTIONAL AND FRAGRANT FRONT DOOR

Transform a narrow hall into an entry that's practical enough for the family and pretty enough for your guests with a hardworking bench-cum–plant stand. Look for a piece that's low enough to sit on, roomy enough to store things under, and wide enough for both drop-and-go items and a few pots. Be careful to consider who uses this space when choosing containers: low, wide, nonbreakable pots (such as the brass vase holding a gardenia plant, opposite, on the right side of the bench) will better serve a bustling family because they won't tip or break.

To re-create this look, choose a long-lasting floor plant, like this 'Alii' ficus (opposite, far left), as a visual anchor for the design. It's a strong focal point that provides a backdrop for the more delicate plants and nicely frames the bench. Then fill the back of the bench with ephemeral, fragrant plants (such as orchids, jasmine, and gardenias). Their wonderful smell will fortify you as you leave and welcome you home upon your return. (After they've finished blooming, put them somewhere less conspicuous where you may care for them until they rebloom—some varieties can even handle being outside.)

A ZEN ENTRY

To turn your entry into a quiet retreat from a busy world, keep your planting simple. Choose soft shapes, a harmonious and subdued color palette, and an unobtrusive container, and be sure to maintain an open path that allows for passing by with ease. This design takes its inspiration from the Saihoji Kokedera (moss temple) garden in Kyoto, which is mostly swaths of green mosses and where visitors instantly feel relaxed upon entering through the garden gates. To mimic that calming experience at home, display a prepotted bonsai tree, or re-create this mini Japanese landscape with a handful of easy-to-find plants.

What You'll Need:

- Ferns and mosses (pictured here: cretan brake fern, Sprengeri fern, spike moss, sheet moss, and mood moss)

- Wide, shallow bowl

- Potting mix

- Smooth, protruding rock

1. Set the plants inside the bowl to plan the layout of the arrangement. Although it is the combination of all the plants that makes the design beautiful, the space that holds the subtle moss ripples is the most impactful feature. Let the tranquil power of the negative space radiate; be thoughtful and add other plants sparingly.

2. Soak the moss in water.

3. Fill the bowl about three-quarters of the way with potting mix—leave enough room so the plants and moss will rest below the rim when they're added.

4. Add a few more scoops of soil and, with cupped hands, mold the soil piles to form tiny mounds.

5. Place the rock off-center in the bowl. Unpot and plant a small fern, tucking it in at the base of the rock as if it grew there naturally.

6. Plant the biggest fern at an angle, letting it drape over the edge of the bowl.

7. Grab clumps of the soaking moss and give each a squeeze to release the water. Gently rest the moss on the soil—mood moss naturally mounds and creates an undulating layer of green, but the mounds give any type of moss a lift. Tuck in a piece of sheet moss or any other kind of moss in the fall of the ripples to create a wave-like moss meadow.

8. To care for the arrangement, keep a spray bottle handy and mist daily with water. Bright or moderate light works well for this planting, but keep it out of direct sun.

This large brass bowl could be considered much too large for a small table, and it would be overpowering if it were filled with big, colorful flowers. But despite the bowl's size, the low mound of greenery inside means it fits the bill here quite nicely.

A LOW-MAINTENANCE, HIGH-STYLE CONSOLE

If a simple-yet-strong style statement with easy-peasy plants is what you're after, 'Janet Craig' compacta dracaena, starfish sansevieria, and 'Fernwood' sansevieria (pictured opposite, on the bottom shelf) are calling your name. These plants tolerate low-light conditions and won't require as frequent watering as many indoor plants. To introduce a rugged touch, stage them in an unconventional vessel like this vintage blacksmith bag (see page 15 for more on staging). To add fragrance and a pop of color to your tabletop, pick up an impressive jewel-tone zygopetalum orchid (top left). These prefer a bit of light (though no direct sun) and weekly watering while in bloom. See below for two more winning options for your entry console.

A Warm Welcome: There's a reason pineapples are often represented on door knockers and welcome mats. They were once a luxurious rarity grown, displayed, and eaten only by the wealthy, who shared them with their most special guests. With such a storied history of hospitality, a potted pineapple plant makes for a fitting addition to your entry. Opt for a sturdy pot that will not only balance the weight of the growing fruit but also complement its color as it evolves from green to yellow. Pineapples need light and moist soil, but the reward goes beyond the symbolic welcome—after the fruit ripens to a golden yellow, cut it off and slice it open for a sweet treat!

Feminine Florals: If you're craving the beauty of a cut floral arrangement but want the ease and enduring quality of a living plant, opt for a blossoming specimen. Greenhouse plant nurseries use patterns of artificial light to trick plants into flowering at "off" times of the year. Their techniques make it easy to pick up *something* in bloom year-round. Here the contrast of the fluffy rosettes of the tuberous begonia and the dark veiny backs of its leaves are oh-so gorgeous. Embrace the fancy, feminine nature of these flowers by choosing an antique-looking pot. Another option: begonia flowers are stunning when snipped and left to float in a bowl of water. Check out more blooming beauties on page 168.

A LIVING CENTERPIECE

If your front door is used only for guests or otherwise isn't called upon to handle shoes and keys and mail, you can create a space that's all about being pretty and welcoming. Think of it as your personal grand hotel lobby and make a splash with it.

The "living centerpiece" shown here is like a flower arrangement, but with live plants. Instead of sharing a pot with other specimens, each plant is kept in its own pot and strategically placed inside the larger main vase, then the pots are covered with moss—a technique called staging. One benefit of staging is that plants with different water requirements can live longer together in the same vase because they can be watered individually. Another benefit is that when an individual plant no longer looks good, you can easily pull it out and pop in another. Though staging arrangements takes time, the outcome is a colorful, eye-catching centerpiece, perfect for a special occasion. Here are the fundamentals for creating your own.

1. Choose a vessel. Pedestal vases allow plants to dangle over their edges for added drama. Lay out the plants, each within its original grow pot, to ensure that the planter is large enough (grow pots are usually made of flexible plastic, so you can squish them a bit to fit them all in).

2. For added height and to prevent leaks, add waterproof stuffing (like Bubble Wrap) to the bottom of extra-deep vases. For another layer of water-leakage protection, set each grow pot inside an individual plastic liner before placing it inside the vase.

3. Think about where the arrangement will live. If it will sit in the open and all its sides will be seen, arrange the plants accordingly. If, however, it will be seen from only one angle, beef up that side and let the unseen area be plain.

4. Add the plants. For a dynamic, vibrant design, keep the viewer's eye moving by arranging your plants in layers. Let one plant rise above the rest (here, the orange-red orchid bloom leads the eye upward). Tuck in other plants at various levels to add movement and liveliness. Create tension by crafting an asymmetrical yet balanced

relationship with the plants (the left side of this arrangement is denser on the top, while the right is heavier on the bottom half).

5. Position some plants at an angle to interrupt the edge of the planter and create a natural look that will appear as if it has been growing there for years.

6. Once you're happy with your composition, fill in any spaces with waterproof stuffing to secure the plants. Add a layer of moss over the top to cover the plastic pots. Water each plant carefully and separately. (A turkey baster works well for this.)

This centerpiece includes (clockwise from the tall, arching orange-red blooms): Catatante orchid, *Tillandsia superinsignis* air plant, calla lily, aquamarine pilea, arrowhead plant, another aquamarine pilea, and hydrangea.

If plants have to be lined up, as they do in this terrarium, vary their height to add dimension and interest. Here a tiny rattan plant stand gave a lemon cypress (left) a boost; the paperwhite blooms (right) will begin to escape out of the opening as they grow taller. Also pictured: parallel peperomia (center).

SAN FRANCISCO CALIFORNIA USA

SHED SOME LIGHT

If you're an apartment dweller with a front door that leads to an interior hallway, or you otherwise have a very low- or no-light entry, consider hanging grow lights. The cheery contraption shown here is a hanging terrarium with programmable LED to mimic the sun, purchased from Modern Sprout's online shop. It gives the impression of a bright window in a windowless room, subliminally connecting viewers to the outdoors, even though it's all a mirage.

To create a similar setup yourself, pick up some full-spectrum LED grow strip lighting (narrow rolls of LED that can be rolled out and adjusted for easy adhesive-strip mounting) and attach the strip (light side downward) to the inside top of a shadow box, upcycled vintage fruit boxes, or any shelving unit. If you purchase a programmable LED unit, set a timer for the electric sunshine: most plants are happy with about twelve hours of light a day, though some sun-loving specimens like succulents need more and others will do well with less. See page 20 for tips on how to know if your plant is getting the right amount of sunlight.

IT'S ALL ABOUT WAVELENGTH

Why can't you use a regular incandescent lightbulb to give plants a boost? Light comes in various colors (wavelengths), and over the course of a day, sunlight goes through the entire color spectrum. The best way to replicate natural conditions for plants in the home is by exposing them to both the cool and warm lights that parallel the natural solar spectrum. Incandescent bulbs emit only the yellow and orange portions of the spectrum, while LEDs produce the full spectrum of light plants need to survive. As a bonus, LEDs' low heat output means you can increase the light intensity by closing the distance between plants and light without burning the leaves.

SMALL SPACE, BIG IMPACT
A VERTICAL GARDEN

If your entryway is a true pass-through, hang a living wall to keep plants in sight but out of the way and save all surface areas—including the floor—for other uses. Re-create the design pictured here using simple shelving brackets and long metal planters with these seven steps.

1. Choose the vessels. These low, long metal troughs can be found at flower shops or home-goods stores, but any lightweight vessels with flat backs will do. These were already lined with plastic, but if yours aren't, waterproof them by lining them with cellophane and/or individual plastic liners.

2. Select the plants. Mix textures, add pops of bright yet related colors, and include a welcoming burst of fragrance. Avoid plants with suckers, such as creeping ficus, ivy, philodendrons, and similar plants if you don't want them climbing up the wall and potentially causing the paint to chip. Here 'Sharry Baby' oncidium orchids, guzmania bromeliads, and jasmine grab the attention, with a combination of fine- and wide-leaved ferns as the backdrop.

3. Design the plantings. Keep the majority of the plants the same from container to container for visual continuity. Let a couple of the containers act as supporting players and keep them simple so that the others can shine for a more compelling design. Make sure the plants' grow pots aren't taller or wider than the vessel (cut off any offending plastic if one is slightly too tall).

4. To visualize where the planters will hang, measure each planter and create actual-size cutouts with scrap paper. Attach the cutouts to the wall with painter's tape, then use the tape to vertically "draw" in a few plants' heights. Step back and take a look. Stand at the front door and take another look. Move the cutouts around until your design is pleasing. For a lush look, hang the vases close to one another and fill the wall with green. Or go for a sparer design with just one or two vessels.

5. Hang each vase with a bracket (ideally, French cleat and a bottom spacer that allows for a plumb hang and ample air flow between the wall and the planter to prevent dampness and mold). It's best if your living wall is easily detachable so you can clean away dust and bugs that linger and hide behind the installation.

6. Set each plant inside the vessel in its original plastic grow pot. If the grow pot is too short, prop it up with something waterproof like Bubble Wrap or an upside-down plastic cup.

7. Follow the care directions for each plant. If ease of care is important to you, be sure to choose plants with similar water and light requirements.

LIVING
ROOM

The living room is one of the most public places in the home and the space where our outward selves reign—the room and its decor are an expression of who we are and what's important to us, plants included. A topiaried tree in a formal living room, for example, might suggest that you like things a bit more controlled, refined, and cared for. The same specimen left to grow wild and woolly might say that you're laid-back and love nature for what it is.

Any size plant is worthy of showing off, but since the living room is often the largest room in the house and tends to have ample floor space, this chapter features lots of big plants, including floor plants and small trees, with tips on how to layer them with a fabulous supporting cast of medium-size green companions.

FLOOR PLANTS

Tall floor plants, meaning plants that grow 5 feet (1.5 m) tall or higher, can serve as visual anchors in your living room in much the same way that trees outdoors form the backbones of garden landscapes. To mimic nature and amplify ceiling height, go as tall as your room allows (see box, page 124) while staying in scale with the surrounding furniture.

Areca Palm

Also called a butterfly palm because of its long, leafy fronds that can exceed 3 feet (1 m) in length, or a golden cane palm due to its towering, bamboo-like stems that can reach up to 8 feet (2.5 m) tall indoors, the areca palm (*Dypsis lutescens*) creates a fresh focal point for the living room. Keep in a brightly lit, humid area, avoiding direct sun. Support healthy new growth by watering liberally in warmer months and reducing the amount in cooler ones (and never let stagnant water sit around its roots).

Fiddle-Leaf Fig

One of the most popular indoor trees, the fiddle-leaf fig (*Ficus lyrata*) may be beloved for its bold, architectural style, but its wavy, paddle-like leaves offer an added benefit: they absorb sound. Keep this multifunctional foliage happy by positioning it in a bright space away from direct sun and allowing the soil to dry out between waterings. Turn to page 46 for another fabulous member of the fig family.

'Lisa' Cane Tree

Meet *Dracaena fragrans* 'Lisa', a strong candidate for almost any low-light room in need of drama. With its long, shiny leaves and staggered green trunks, the cane tree adapts perfectly to average home conditions and needs little extra attention to thrive. Light shade makes for great growing conditions—an east- or west-facing window is an ideal spot. Keep the soil evenly moist, reducing watering in winter but never letting it dry out completely. For a dracaena with patterned leaves, see page 42.

Umbrella Tree

The schefflera plant is commonly called either the umbrella tree or octopus tree, which gives a clue to its character: its unusually shaped leaves radiate out from its stem like spokes or tentacles. Generally undemanding additions to the home, both *Schefflera actinophylla* 'Amate' and the dwarf umbrella plant (*S. arboricola*; pictured here) favor bright light, which will ensure that they retain their fullness. To keep the foliage of *S. aboricola* dense, pinch off the top few leaves to promote new growth at the base.

A STATEMENT-MAKING SYMMETRICAL ARRANGEMENT

In this modern, masculine living room, a few well-chosen plants add life and warmth, creating a space where people will feel at ease. A formal, symmetrical pairing of towering foxtail palms in matching industrial planters flanks the couch, with a coffee table (topped with a nerve plant) centered between the planters and little else in the way of adornment, emphasizing the bold cleanliness of the design.

There's more to a well-balanced space than the physical arrangements of the objects in the room. You want to balance the *feeling* of the space as well. Though the size and placement of the foxtail palms telegraph strength and power, their curved stems frame the couch to create a canopy that softens the look and adds much-needed coziness and comfort to the room. Similarly, the dark colors of the couch and metal planters needed to be offset with some lightness: elevating the plants provides negative space and lifts the "weight" off the floor. Finally, a repeated triangular pattern woven through the room's design (in the lattice of the metal coffee table, the artwork, the leaf shape of the foxtails, and the knitted throw) ties the whole look together.

HIGH CEILINGS CALL FOR TALL PLANTS

Floor plants should reach up to, but not touch, the ceiling. A tall plant resting several feet below the ceiling will draw the eye down rather than up, making the space feel cavernous instead of generous. If your plant isn't tall enough on its own, you can add a plant stand—or place a sturdy block of wood under the tree's grow pot and liner within its larger cachepot—to get the height you need.

AN ECLECTIC ASYMMETRICAL ARRANGEMENT

The beauty of an asymmetrical look like this one is the way a viewer's eye moves gently across the scene, from the oversize fiddle-leaf fig on the left to the intricately patterned specimens under the coffee table to the yucca peeking out from behind the couch. There's a rhythm to it all—and a balance. The arrangement is anchored by the center "unit" of the couch, coffee table, and set of art prints. From that foundation, the height of the fig on the left is offset by the relative mass of the plants on the right. More greenery and decor were then easily added to this well-balanced design.

The whole scene is unified by a common palette: the pots are made from natural materials (wood, rattan, and marble), and many of the plants themselves have a similar dusty pink hue, which adds a touch of femininity to the space. *For a complete list of plants featured in this room, turn to page 272.*

PLANTS, PLANTS EVERYWHERE!

For a layered design, tuck plants into unexpected places. Here are a few tips.

- **Create a backdrop.** Use the space behind a sofa to display floor plants or plants set on a table or plant stand.

- **Add interest close to the ground.** Place a plant next to or slightly under a table, for example, or at the corner of a bookcase or couch.

- **Think beyond the plant stand.** Create a tower of books and use it to lift a plant to just the right height.

STANDOUTS FOR THE COFFEE TABLE

The coffee table is a key complement to your couch, perfect for resting teacups or your stocking feet on. This is a high-traffic space, and real estate on the table is precious. When adding a plant, it's best to keep things simple. Here are a few options.

Keep It Low

For a low-profile plant that won't topple over, place a draping specimen like this 'Hope' peperomia in a large, shallow bowl. Let its waxy leaves gently tumble over the edge of the container and table. Here the peperomia's root-ball is wrapped in moss, a practice called kokedama. Once a week, soak the moss in water and gently squeeze out the excess before returning the plant to the bowl. (See page 18 for more on kokedama.)

Stack 'Em Up

Succulents like this Devotion echeveria are often found at grocery store chains planted in simple terra-cotta pots. Rather than repotting it or tucking it into a cachepot, why not simply stack the terra-cotta container on top of other decorative bowls? This quirky styling trick comes with a bonus: the bowls will prevent any excess water or moisture from damaging the table, and they can even be repurposed as temporary coasters for your drinks!

Shadowy Show-Offs

In the right light, a sculptural plant like this sago palm creates exceptional patterns on walls, floors, and tables. This can be achieved with either direct sun from the window or a lamp strategically positioned to spotlight the leaves. Shine some light on the geometric leaf holes of the Swiss cheese vine or a strappy ponytail palm for two other intriguing shadow patterns.

Sheer Beauty

Some plants' leaves, like those of this 'Escargot' begonia, are even more marvelous when backlit. This moody combination of a warm, brassy wood table, dark walls, and the begonia set in a wooden bowl makes for a sumptuous scene. The sheer, speckled leaves of caladiums also interact beautifully with light, and the patterns of thicker marbled leaves of bromeliads and veined alocasias are enhanced by a bit of sunshine.

FIREPLACE FOLIAGE

Whether it's fired up or left cold, a fireplace is a prominent feature in any room lucky enough to have one. From a beautiful marble mantelpiece to a simple wood-burning oven, the hearth makes a dramatic stage for a collection of plants.

Country Haven

To create a "mantel" for this rustic, unfinished fireplace, a large lichen-covered branch was hung from the ceiling with fishing line. Lichen is a living combination of algae and fungus: mist now and again to keep it alive. A stool propping up a container of spike moss (left) and some grape hyacinth blooms (right) completes this eclectic, woodsy tableau.

Modern Verdure

A sunny chartreuse print and bright green foliage enliven this striking all-white fireplace setup. On the mantel, a prickly but lovable 'Dinni Yellow' crown of thorns plant is balanced by a trio of candlesticks. Inside the fireplace, the patterned leaves of a prayer plant complement the herringbone tile—a far cheerier addition than a stack of logs!

A ROTATING MANTEL

The principles of feng shui call for nine healthy plants to be placed on or around your fireplace, as their life force is seen as a necessary balance to the surrounding fire energy. Though finding space for nine plants around your hearth all at once may be a tall order, here is a cast of characters you can rotate throughout the year.

Early Spring Blooms

Whether you've grown them from bulbs or picked up a pot of ready-to-bloom specimens, paperwhites provide a pop of fragrance and beauty when little else is growing. For a longer-lasting display, tuck in an air plant (such as this *Tillandsia xerographica*).

A Burst of Citrus

Create an ephemeral display for your mantel by gathering a bundle of seasonal fruit still attached to its branches, like this citrus, and placing it on a tray. Since they aren't in water, the leaves will dry in a day or two (and eventually the fruit will shrivel—unless you eat it first!).

A Rustic Combination

The rich, autumnal colors of these plants (from left to right: 'Red Ripple' peperomia, creeping wire vine, and mum) need little in the way of added decoration. Simply wrap their grow pots in brown paper and twine and drop them into a waterproofed wooden container.

Winter Wonderland

Create a "snowy mound" of Spanish moss and top with snowflakelike succulent cuttings and air plants. (Succulent cuttings are the snipped heads of grown plants.) This low-maintenance display will last through the season, depending on the succulent choice (some, like this 'Lola' echeveria, can survive a month or more).

Use shadow boxes to display and frame plants. Get in close and watch the leaves of this resurrection plant (in the glass box) unfold when it's watered.

TAKE THE FOCUS
OFF THE TV

Create a jungle of plants around your entertainment center to keep the TV from dominating your living room. The key is to set the scene, not steal it. You want to be able to clearly see and focus on the television when it's on, so your plants should frame, but not overlap, the screen. Though there is a *lot* going on here, the backdrop is so full and the foliage and pots sufficiently unified in palette that it all blends into a pleasing wall of green. Big, colorful blooms or lots of empty spaces on the wall would fight for attention. *For a complete list of plants featured in this room, turn to page 272.*

A CORNER FOR RETREAT

Create a special corner in your home that is all about you—a place to nourish your body and mind. What do you want to see and how do you want to feel when you're sitting there? Do you yearn for a cozy nook where you can sit quietly, beside a plant or two? Or do you crave an open and airy space to instill a sense of calm? Here are a few styles to choose from.

3

1. Sleek

An iconic Eames lounge chair calls for an equally architectural plantscape, like this pencil cactus in a simple concrete pot (left). Because we're more comfortable seated in a space with a protected back— open spaces behind us leave us feeling vulnerable— the alpine schefflera behind the chair creates an increased feeling of security and adds needed height to the display.

2. Tranquil

Everything about this spare look says "breathe": the soothing colors of the chair, the smooth shape of the beige vase, and the translucent, flowing curtain (which also provides the filtered light necessary for the elephant ear plant). The upright stems and beautiful fan-shaped leaves of the elephant ear look as though they're ready to cool you off. *Ahhhh.*

3. Mod

Travel back in time with this candy-red couch, geometric pillow, and out-of-the-ordinary fishbone cactus hung from leather straps in a repurposed birdcage stand. This elevated arrangement is perfect if you have limited floor space or want to create a vertical garden without making holes in your wall.

LET YOUR SPACE
TELL YOUR STORY

If your living room has a bookshelf, turn it into an open display case that communicates who you are and what is most meaningful to you. Alongside your books, heirlooms, baseball trophies, and family photos, sprinkle in some plants that give you as much joy as these mementos. It adds up to a sense of place that makes your house a home and your living room a room for living. Here's how to pull it all together.

Pick favorites. Identify one piece you love and go from there. The leather chair here influences all the other details in this corner, from the stitching detail along the rim of the succulent dish (on the side table) to the rivet details on the large brass cachepot holding the rubber plant (far left).

Choose a color palette. Using your main piece as a guide, select a few key colors for your space and repeat, repeat, repeat. Leathery browns dominate here, from the dark rubber plant (far left) to the coppery color of the begonia (second shelf, right) and the copper vase with the maidenhair fern (bottom shelf).

Intermingle plants and objects. Your collection will look more unified if your chosen artwork and ephemera are interacting with the plants (like the ferns "growing" out of the vintage mushrooms on the second shelf, left). Or turn your plants *into* objects for display by putting them under a cloche (as in the miniature 'Needlepoint' English ivy on the third shelf).

Create an engaging composition. The glory bower (draping from above) and begonia (second shelf, right) interrupt the "lines" of the shelves and help guide the eye up and down the display.

A GREEN
ROOM DIVIDER

Living rooms come in all shapes and sizes. If yours is open and a bit cavernous, up the cozy factor and create two rooms in a flash with a modular bookshelf decked out with plants. The divider shown here provides some privacy but is still airy enough to keep the whole space feeling connected. The best part is that both the shelf unit and the plants are easily movable if your needs change or your style evolves.

To keep things open, add low, drapey plants that allow a view through to the other side of the divider. A glass terrarium and neutral-colored pottery help keep the shelving unit looking spacious. *For a complete list of plants featured in this room, turn to page 272.*

A 360° View: Remember, the plants and objects on your divider will be seen from both sides. This bonsai 'Partita' begonia was carefully pruned from all angles so it looks good from any vantage point. If you position a plant so that it is facing in one direction, place another so that it faces in the opposite direction. This way, you'll get a unique, attractive view from each side.

The variegated leaf patterns on the plants next to the couch and those on the shelving unit help tie the two spaces together.

FRAME YOUR VIEW

Some windows look out on glorious rolling hills, others onto
bustling streets and skyscrapers—but whatever the view, those
glass panes are your home's connection to the outside world.
Accessorize your outdoor scenery with a planted "frame" to
bridge the gap between outdoors and in. The alcove of this
bay window is a study in how a grouping of plants can add
up to more than the sum of its parts: The variegated African
candelabra cactus (left) and a small fancy-leaf zonal geranium
(center) make for a fine pair in their coordinating pedestal
stands, but they'd look lonely if they were the only greenery
in this large alcove. A modern planter (in a similar style and
complementary tone; right) holding two aloe plants as well as
a draping begonia and an olive plant adds some needed weight
to the right side of the alcove, and the scene is finished with a
hanging 'Attar of Roses' pelargonium that is just the right size
for the central window. For a simpler framing device, seek out
an arching potted tree. Place it so the trunk fills one side of the
window and the branch curves along the top, creating a simple
frame to draw the eye to the view outside.

DISGUISE YOUR VIEW

If your window looks onto a less-than-picturesque scene, a rowdy mix of eye-catching plants is just the thing to draw attention away from the not-so-great outdoors. Put a lot of plants on display with a tiered plant stand—position those that require the most light on top, transitioning to shade lovers on the bottom. Grouping plants also has the added benefit of creating humidity for those that require higher-than-average air moisture.

Consider each plant in relation to the whole grouping, combining a mix of colors and textures. Here the purple-and-white flowers of the tiny dancing Cape primrose (middle tier, right) are accented by the bright yellow strapping leaves of the kiwi dragon tree below it, and the bold leaf of the showy medinilla (floor, center) next to the finer details of the Ming aralia (foreground, left) make for a composition where each plant stands out instead of blending into a tangled mess. Here are a few more lessons to be learned from this collection.

Twirl a lazy Susan. This kitchen standby is super handy as a plant stand: here it holds a showy medinilla and is rotated regularly to encourage even growth.

Go lightweight. Plastic pots are much easier on the back, and thanks to a new crop of designers, they're easy on the eyes, too, with a wide range of colors and appealing shapes and styles. They're especially useful as a counterpoint to "overweight" and awkward plants like this Napoleon's hat (right).

Repurpose. Hang a vintage birdcage and grow a jasmine vine inside it. Or conceal an ugly grow pot in an ordinary canvas tote.

Incorporate your watering can. Keep your watering can handy to make caring for your plants a snap. Choose one that's stylish enough, and you'll be happy to have it as part of the scene.

Embrace happy accidents. Be careful when potting a burro's tail (hanging, right) or baby burro's tail (hanging, center)—the tiny succulents' leaves tend to fall off with the slightest nudge. The upside to this is that you can root the fallen leaves—simply set them atop a pot of soil and keep in moderate light; with patience, they'll begin to sprout.

For a complete list of plants featured in this room, turn to page 272.

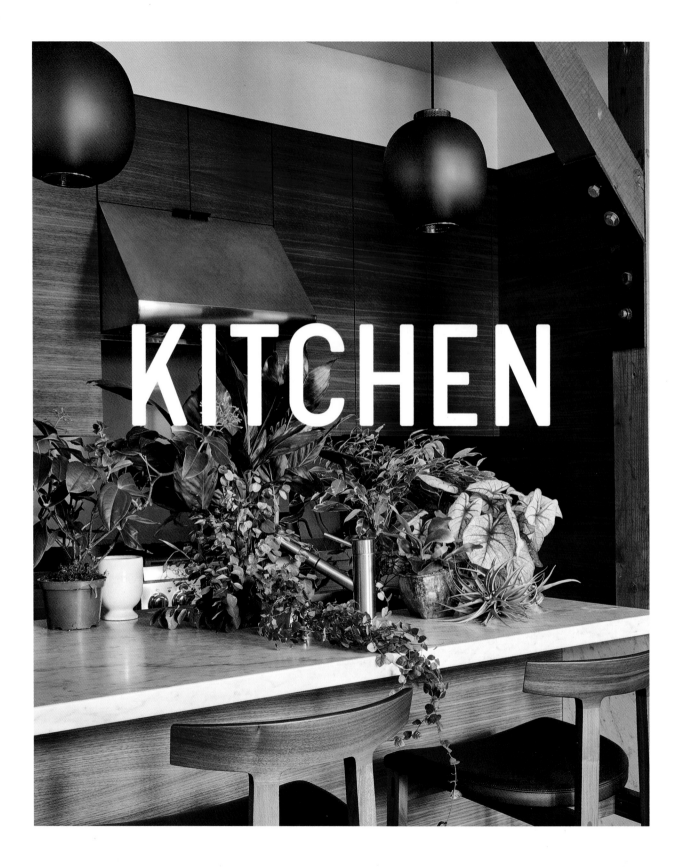

he kitchen is the heart of the home. It's where people gather, cook, and nourish one another. It's also among the most convenient places to keep plants: with wipeable countertops and sweepable floors, there's a lot less worry about water damage or mess—and, of course, there's always a water source at the ready (simply soak the plants in a filled sink or give them a sprinkle with the faucet). This is a hardworking room, so in the pages that follow you'll find plants that can be put to use (including specimens that are good to eat and helpful in controlling pests) and ideas for keeping green things off the countertops and out of the way.

HERBS

Whether set on your windowsill or hanging from the rafters, herbs are an obvious choice for the kitchen. They look pretty, can be used in cooking, and smell great (even if you're just making a sandwich nearby). Here are just a few of the many herbs that grow well indoors—to start choose ones you'll enjoy cooking with, so you'll have the satisfaction of using what you grow. Then turn to pages 150–151 for some easy solutions for keeping these plants in your kitchen.

Lemongrass

The tropical fountain of this Asian cooking staple rivals many ornamental grasses in appearance and carries a citrusy fragrance to boot. Use the tender green base of the stem in stir-fries and curries or infuse leaves for tea. With a preference for direct light, lemongrass (*Cymbopogon citratus*) makes an exotic addition to a sunny windowsill; ensure that the soil remains damp but not soggy. Harvest regularly to promote new growth, and if you find yourself with more than you know what to do with, dry or freeze it to always have some on hand.

Thyme

Greeks burned thyme as a tribute to their gods, and medieval warriors believed that bathing in it would bestow courage. Pictured here is golden variegated lemon thyme (*Thymus × citriodorus* 'Aureus'), but there are more than sixty varieties and counting, so choose one that appeals to you. Thyme is a natural partner for vegetable and chicken dishes; it gives a refreshing lift to a pot of tea; and, when crushed, its oils make for a quick and easy homemade mosquito repellant. Give the plant direct sun or at least six hours of bright light each day, and water when the top inch (2.5 cm) of soil dries out.

MORE EDIBLE PLANTS THAT CAN THRIVE INDOORS

- Arabian coffee (*Coffea arabica*)

- Cilantro (*Coriandrum sativum*)

- Culinary sage (*Salvia officinalis*)

- Curry leaf (*Murraya koenigii*)

- Ginger root (*Zingiber officinale*)

- Marjoram (*Origanum morjorana*)

- Parsley (*Petroselinum crispum*)

- Peppermint (*Mentha × piperita*)

- Rosemary (*Rosmarinus officinalis*)

- Sweet bay laurel (*Laurus nobilis*)

- Turmeric (*Curcuma longa*)

- Watercress (*Nasturtium officinale*)

Basil

We all know basil is the perfect partner for juicy tomatoes. The ubiquitous green variety is often found for sale at grocery stores in both bundles and as growing plants. This blue variety—African blue basil (*Ocimum kilimandscharicum*)— may not be found at your local grocery, but it is worth seeking out for its deep violet blooms and striking stems. It does best in direct light and should be kept away from drafts in winter months. Keep the soil moist but not soggy, and be sure to plant in a pot with a drainage hole.

Oregano

The Greeks referred to both oregano (*Origanum vulgare*) and marjoram (*Origanum majorana*) as "joy of the mountain." In Greek mythology, Aphrodite created oregano as a symbol of happiness. Its pungent, peppery essence intensifies when it is dried (see page 151 for tips on drying your herbs). For optimal growth, let the direct sun hit the plant and water only when the soil feels dry to the touch.

HERB SAVERS

Whether you are starting with just a single plant or are a culinary master who wants a wide range of flavors at your fingertips, here are a few simple ways to grow and store herbs in your kitchen.

Stage

To house your herbs the easy way, keep them in their grow pots and stage them in a decorative cachepot. The box shown at left, made by Smith & Hawken, fits three 4-inch (10 cm) grow pots perfectly and is outfitted with a tray to catch any extra water. The blue bowl (from Heath Ceramics) is home to a strawberry plant. Pop pots in and out as the seasons change— or as culinary inspiration strikes!

Hang

Repurpose an old kitchen standby, the multitiered fruit basket, into your own hanging herb garden. Pair with inexpensive terra-cotta pots, painted in the colors of your choosing as an added upgrade. Pictured here is a mix of mint, thyme, and sage (top tier) and a combination of basil and oregano (bottom tier). Grown more for looks than flavor, 'Kent Beauty' oregano is the perfect hanging plant, as it offers up pendulous flowers with a profuse fragrance.

Cut

After buying fresh-cut herbs at the market, give the bottoms of the stems a fresh snip, fill a vase with cool water, and place the herbs inside. Remove any leaves that are underwater to help keep the water clear. This multimouthed vase allows you to separate each herb into its own slot rather than wrestle with a hodgepodge of greens. Although this storage method is more temporary than keeping a potted plant, cut herbs can stay fresh for a week or more if you change the water often and keep them out of direct sun—and during this time, they will fill your kitchen with their alluring fragrances!

Dry

Give cut herbs a longer life—and add a colorful display to your kitchen wall—by hanging them to dry. Bundle and hang herbs upside down for a few weeks, then store in an airtight container out of direct light and use within a few months (their flavor will gradually fade). Pictured here is oregano (top row) and (bottom row, from left to right) mint, rosemary, red chile pepper, white sage, and lavender. If you'd like to keep the herbs on display, I find that oregano, sage, and thyme dry more beautifully than rosemary and basil. The "drying rack" shown here is actually a simple wooden dish rack.

CLEAR YOUR COUNTERTOPS

If space is tight, or you just want to add a bit of interest to your walls, here are two ways to elevate your potted plants. They will be heavy, especially after they've been watered, so make sure that whatever hanging style you select, you drill into a stud or use a wall anchor.

Wall Hook

This vintage "woven" metal cachepot is the perfect foil to the large, simple shapes of *Hoya obovata* planted in a simple terra-cotta pot. The pretty copper hook it's hanging from is from Terrain, but you could easily paint a generic hardware-store hook whatever tone you'd like. After installing your hook, measure the radius of the pot you'd like to hang (the length from the center to one of its edges) and compare that to the distance from the end of the hook to the wall to be sure there is enough clearance. Care tip: If you're often sautéing on your stovetop, your plants may soon bear a layer of kitchen grime. Keep them clean by gently wiping them occasionally with a damp, soft rag.

Loop Hanger

This iron loop hanger (readily available in garden sections of hardware stores) conjures up images of brightly colored pelargoniums hanging en masse on the side of an old French farmhouse. But who says it has to be used outside? To complete the rustic vibe, plant your specimen in a simple terra-cotta pot. Here the Swedish ivy (*Plectranthus ciliatus*) was kept in its original grow pot and placed into the terra-cotta container (which was itself lined in plastic) to prevent dirty water from dripping onto the counter after watering.

LOW LIGHT, NO PROBLEM

If your kitchen doesn't get much direct light, fear not! There are still plenty of fabulous plants that can liven up your shelf. Choose a few that are right for you, then brighten up the display by potting them in white and neutral-toned vessels. Avoid overcrowding the shelves—an airy, spare arrangement will help the space feel open and light. Here are a few low-light-friendly plants to consider.

1. Ivy: Almost any ivy can handle low-light conditions. Some, like this 'Teardrop' English ivy variety (*Heldera helix* 'Teardrop'), like to crawl and may stick to nearby surfaces. Let some strands dangle to add movement to your shelf. Ivies are generally easy to care for, but they do require some humidity. Solid green varieties like this one are known to grow more easily indoors, but they come in yellow and white variegated leaf patterns as well.

2. Low-Light Fern: Ferns are thought to have been among the first plants on earth. Their low-maintenance nature and adaptability mean they're still easily found today. Unlike most plants, which reproduce using flowers and seeds, ferns create more ferns via spores on the undersides of their fronds. This blue star fern (*Phlebodium aureum*) is laid-back—just keep it moist and it will be happy.

3. Marimo: Native to cool lake bottoms, marimo (*Aegagropila linnaei*) prefer low light. For a kitchen-specific twist, plop one in a spice jar–turned-aquarium! Change the water every few weeks and give the ball a gentle squeeze periodically to help maintain its round shape.

4. Baby Rubber Plant: The name baby rubber plant is a misnomer for *Peperomia obtusifolia*: this member of the peperomia family is not a rubber plant at all and is more closely related to the black pepper plant. Pictured here is *P. obtusifolia* 'Marble', whose thick, upright stems hold large marbled leaves that eventually take on a bushy appearance. It thrives in moderate to bright light but like all peperomia (see page 68) is extremely forgiving and will take lower light with ease. Allow the soil to dry between waterings.

AN EXOTIC COMBINATION PLANTER

Orchids are incredible plants—they come in so many fun colors, and some bloom for a month or more. This apricot-peach-pink Surf Song orchid (a relative of the phalaenopsis orchid—see page 58) looks like a vibrant tropical sunset. Combine this stunner with a mix of supporting foliage (all kept in their original grow pots). Disassemble the planter once the orchid blooms fade or if the succulent grows leggy, reaching for more light. Otherwise, keep the plants together for a long-lasting foliage arrangement.

1. Lay out the plants, each in its original grow pot, and ensure that your bowl is bigger than the group of plants to be placed inside (grow pots are usually made of flexible plastic, so you can squish them a bit to fit them in).

2. Decide where the bowl will live. If it will be seen from all sides, arrange the plants accordingly. If, however, it will be seen from only one angle, beef up that side and let the unseen area be plain. Set the orchid first, then tuck in other plants around it to fill out the arrangement. If you are using a watertight plastic bowl, prevent extra water from swimming around the bottom by placing each grow pot inside an individual plastic liner before fitting it inside the container. As you work, stabilize the arrangement inside the bowl with Bubble Wrap.

3. Once you're happy with your composition, fill in any remaining spaces with Bubble Wrap. Add a layer of moss to cover the plastic pots. Water each plant carefully and separately—the succulent, for example, requires less watering than the nerve plant.

What You'll Need:

- Surf Song orchid (*Doritaenopsis* 'Kumquat')
- 'Tricolor' fern (*Pteris quadriaurita* 'Tricolor')
- Nerve plant (*Fittonia albivenis* Verschaffeltii Group)
- 'Perle von Nürnberg' echeveria (*Echeveria* 'Perle von Nürnberg')
- Vriesea bromeliad (*Vriesea ospinae* var. *gruberi*)
- Salad bowl or appropriate-size vessel
- Individual plastic liners (optional)
- Bubble Wrap or waterproof stuffing
- Sheet moss, mood moss, or any other type of moss

A FORAGED POT-ET-FLEUR

Pot-et-fleur, a style of flower arranging fashionable in the Victorian era, features houseplants that are combined with cut flowers and foliage to create spectacular, ever-changing centerpieces. For this wintery pot-et-fleur arrangement, the singular stalk of a blooming hippeastrum keeps company with a mix of foraged stems. Head into the woods to find a few branches from a woody shrub (these will be stronger and easier to jam into the soil) as well as some greenery, ideally specimens that will dry well. Shown here are stems of heavenly bamboo, which will get a bit "crunchy" over time but should hold up until the hippeastrum has finished blooming (if you're willing to be patient, the bulb *will* rebloom—see page 49 for instructions). Holiday greens such as pine and cedar are also good options and are readily available for purchase in November and December if foraging isn't an option.

What You'll Need:

- Plastic liner
- Decorative vessel
- Hippeastrum
- Foraged branches and greens
- Garden snips
- Sheet moss, mood moss, or any other type of moss

1. To prevent leaks, add waterproof lining to the bottom of your chosen vessel. Then position the hippeastrum in the vessel, keeping it in its original grow pot.

2. Trim your foraged branches to 12 to 16 inches (30 to 41 cm) in length.

3. Prep your greenery by removing the leaves from the bottom few inches (7.5 cm) of each stem, then tuck them into the soil around the bulb of your hippeastrum. Add the branches to create height in the arrangement.

4. Fill in any gaps and cover the cachepot with moss, and you're done!

PEST CONTROL

While most plants acquire nutrients through their roots, carnivorous plants have developed techniques to lure insects into their "pitchers," trap them with their sticky pads, and suck them down their slippery leaves. As the insects decay, the plant soaks up all their nutrients. Sounds like a science project, huh? The Venus flytrap is certainly the most famous carnivorous plant, but there are other bizarre and beautiful specimens that make for prehistoric-looking, practical displays as well.

1

2

1. Monkey Cups

Monkey cups (*Nepenthes* spp.) are naturally found in tropical rain-forest canopies, where they catch water and bugs from the sky (and where monkeys can enjoy a drink from their pitchers—thus their funny name). These plants love humidity and should be kept damp at all times. Unlike their sun-loving carnivorous companion the pitcher plant (see below), they do not like direct sun.

2. Pitcher Plant

Pitcher plants (*Sarracenia* spp.; left) can be found in both short varieties that grow to just a few inches (7.5 cm) high and taller ones that can reach up to 30 inches (76 cm). Pair your pest controller with another hardworking kitchen favorite, an Arabian coffee plant (*Coffea arabica*; right). With patience and a whole lot of light, these evergreen plants will produce raw coffee beans (in three to five years).

3. Sundew

The sundew (*Drosera* spp.) is a bog plant and prefers a wet environment. Here pebbles and moss were added to polish off the top attractively. Place the sundew in a bright place and keep it moist, and this wondrous kitchen companion will lure fruit flies and other pests and wow your family and friends.

STELLAR SILLS

Even the narrowest of windowsills can hold a few plants and bring life to your kitchen. Remember, though, that this area is often susceptible to the outside environment—winters can be cold and drafty, and summers can get quite hot. Move your friends out of these extremes as needed.

Low-Light Stunners

This lineup of tried-and-true low-light plants gets extra zing from an eclectic mix of containers in varying materials and shapes. The tallest specimens are housed in mugs of roughly matching heights (at far left, a ZZ plant; center, a spear sansevieria). A pair of short ceramic saltcellars was repurposed to hold a 'Red Ripple' peperomia (second from left) and haworthia (far right)—the plants themselves were placed at a slant to match the containers' profiles. The only "real" pot here is a teeny-tiny vessel holding a teeny-tiny ivy (second from right).

Mix-and-Match Sunny Succulents

A brightly lit windowsill calls for a wild menagerie of succulents. If space is at a premium, gather your favorites into a single mug—pictured here are watch chain, variegated corncob cactus, 'Lola' echeveria, thimble cactus, and Siebold's stonecrop. The plants' muted tones mean the variety of shapes and textures is the focus. Keep your collection growing by plucking or snipping any offshoots—simply set them on some soil to root and watch them thrive.

WATCH IT GROW

Most fruits and vegetables require too much space or sunlight to successfully grow indoors, but both microgreens and sprouts are great options for your own indoor vegetable patch! They need very little space to grow, and they are easy and superfast to harvest. In a matter of days, you'll have a nutrition-packed snack growing right on your kitchen counter.

MICROGREENS

Think of microgreens as mini versions of your favorite veggies—they are the first shoots and tiny leaves that grow from the vegetables' seeds. They are packed with vitamins and minerals—up to forty times more than their mature selves—and have a stronger flavor than sprouts. A wide range of vegetables can be enjoyed as delicious microgreens, including broccoli, kale, radish, and garden peas (pictured here). The directions below are specifically for pea shoots, but many microgreens are grown similarly.

1. Pick up a microgreen seed packet at your local plant nursery or natural foods store or online. Soak the seeds in water for twenty-four hours in a cool place.

2. Scatter the seeds over a container of moist potting mix, water very lightly, and cover with a thin layer of soil.

3. Cover with plastic wrap or a plastic tray to keep the soil warm and encourage germination. Remove once shoots become visible.

4. After three days, shoots will appear. Remove the cover and water daily. Shoots will bend toward the light, so rotate the tray to keep the crop straight.

5. When the new growth reaches 4 to 8 inches (10 to 20 cm) tall, have two sets of leaves per shoot, and are about to topple, it's time to harvest. (This usually happens ten to twenty days after sowing.) To harvest, cut the stems just above the soil line, rinse, and use immediately or store in the refrigerator for up to three days. They sometimes regrow, especially if planted in a larger container.

SPROUTS

As with microgreens, there are many types of sprouts—the germinated seeds of a wide variety of foods, including legumes, grains, nuts, and more. Wheat berries (pictured here) are chewy and nutty and make a great addition to salads and soups. They grow in low-light, moist environments and don't require any soil. Best of all, they'll be ready to eat in just four to six days. Here's how to grow your own:

1. Select a seed packet from a local plant nursery or natural foods store or online. Place 4 tablespoons of dry sprout seeds in a bowl and rinse until the water runs clear.

2. Add enough water to cover the seeds by 1 inch (2.5 cm) and let soak for eight to twelve hours in a cool place.

3. Pour off the soaking water and gently rinse the seeds with room-temperature water. Pour the seeds into a sprouter (a special device for germinating grains); alternatively, place seeds inside a clean quart-size glass jar, cover with cheesecloth, and secure the cloth with a rubber band. Allow excess water to drain out. If you are using a jar, you may want to place it at a 45-degree angle when pouring out the excess water, then hold it upside down for a few minutes to ensure that all excess water is removed.

4. Rinse the sprouts at least twice daily with room-temperature water, draining out the water each time.

5. Sprouts are ready to eat when they are 1 to 2 inches (2.5 to 5 cm) long (usually four to six days after starting). Rinse one more time, ensure that they are dry to the touch (use a salad spinner or pat dry with a clean dish towel or paper towels), and store them in the refrigerator. They should keep, refrigerated, for up to a week.

DINING
ROOM

The dining room table is an expression of community: a place to gather; to celebrate life, family, and friendship; to share the good stuff. Whether you're blowing out birthday candles with a circle of friends or recapping the day's events over a steaming plate of eggplant parmigiana, create a warm and inviting space where people want to connect, not eat and run. In the pages that follow, you'll find easy-peasy table settings and more extravagant, showy plant combinations. Some can remain on your table long after your dinner party, while others are more ephemeral: move them around, replant them inside or out, mix them up, even give them away. Like a good meal, plants nourish us and are meant to be shared.

FLOWERING PLANTS

Flowers make us smile. It's a scientific fact! Studies have shown that flowers produce zygomatic muscle activity (smiles) in humans, and researchers have concluded that flowers are using us to help them thrive—they charm us so we'll love them, care for them, and help them live. After all, iris bulbs don't divide themselves! The flowering plants below are particularly well suited to dining rooms, where they can serve as festive, long-lasting centerpieces.

Hellebore

The hellebore (*Helleborus* spp.), an early-spring bloomer that can be found peeking out of the snow in outdoor gardens, is also called the Christmas or Lenten rose. Believed in ancient times to cure madness, these plants are actually poisonous. A foil to their rugged, thick leaves, their saucer-shaped flowers (in chartreuse green to mauve tones, and even frilly double blooms) are oh-so demure. Keep them cool and let the soil dry out slightly between waterings.

Hydrangea

Hydrangea is Greek for "water vessel"—a fitting name because this guy likes things wet! Although hydrangea are unlikely to survive year-round indoors, you can take a few steps to keep them at their best before relocating them to the garden in spring. Remove the foil wrapper (if it came in one, as the Magic Carousel *Hydrangea macrophylla* pictured here often does) to allow for drainage, place the plant in moderate to bright light, and check the soil for moisture each day while it's blooming (aim for a constantly moist, but not soggy, medium).

Calandiva

This low-maintenance cultivar of the well-known succulent flaming Katy (Calandiva *Kalanchoe blossfeldiana*) can keep its brightly colored yellow, red, pink, or orange double blooms for a full six weeks through winter. Allow the soil to dry out between waterings, then water thoroughly and situate in a spot with moderate to bright light. To get your plant blooming again the following year, for six weeks beginning in September, move the plant to an area with fourteen to sixteen hours of complete darkness each night and with bright light during the day; by October or November, you should see buds forming again.

Chenille Plant

Cascades of crimson catkins (flowers that look like tassels) animate the heart-shaped foliage of this weirdly elegant draping plant. The common name chenille plant refers to two different species: *Acalypha hispida*, with foxtail-like blooms, and *A. pendula*, pictured here (which is also commonly called strawberry firetails). Both require year-round warm temperatures and bright conditions for continual flowering. They are fast-growing specimens so they need copious amounts of water, but let the soil get dry between waterings.

At the left end of the table, a halved seedpod is a home for a stand-alone China doll plant as well as a fern that is tucked into the top of the planted vase (tilted slightly to let the fronds airily dangle off the edge).

Supporting Cast: Tiger branches are a textural, practical addition to the arrangement: they hold up the head of an oversize orchid bloom so it won't droop.

A TROPICAL VIEW

Turn your dining room into an ocean paradise with chartreuse Bulldog-type paphiopedilum orchids (in stages from bud to full bloom) and aqua-blue accents, complemented by a lively backdrop that includes ferns, spike moss, a zebra plant, an aluminum plant, and a moody, black-leaved 'Black Beauty' imperial taro. The weathered copper troughs play into the color scheme as well—as copper tarnishes, it turns a lovely bluish hue. The theme is repeated, with a slight twist, in the smaller arrangement on the side table: plants in a similar palette (including another paphiopedilum orchid, also seen on page 60) mimic but do not exactly replicate the design of the tablescape. Keep these arrangements moist, cool, and out of direct sun. The orchids should bloom for about a month. When they've finished blooming, snip off the spent flowers and stems and enjoy the green scene or take apart and repot each plant.

A WOODLAND KOKEDAMA TABLESCAPE

Dining table centerpieces should be striking and noticeable from afar, and interesting but unobtrusive when guests are seated at the table. All these style goals are accomplished with this forest-themed tablescape. No vases are required for this living centerpiece. Because each plant is in its own moss "wrapper," the whole arrangement is incredibly flexible—and at the end of the evening, it can be disassembled so each guest can be given a living memento of the evening. Turn the page to learn how to re-create this look.

1. Create individual kokedama using your moss and mix of small plants, following the instructions on page 18. Use 5-inch (12 cm) pieces of moss for your 2-inch (5 cm) plants and 8-inch (20 cm) pieces for each 4-inch (10 cm) plant.

2. Set cork bark pieces in the center of the table, leaving enough room for glasses and plates. In the photo on the preceding page, two are staggered and overlapped to create a natural shape.

3. Place the moss-wrapped plants on the logs, reserving a small kokedama for each place setting. Think about your guests' views: rest some plants at an angle so they peek out at the guest facing them. Cluster some plants and leave others single.

4. If you like, stick a candle adhesive dot to the bottom of each candle and firmly press onto the logs, or just melt the candle a bit and drip it on the bark to hold it in place.

Tip: If purchasing your sheet moss prepackaged from a craft store, be aware that its lovely bright green dye job may bleed green onto your hands or your tablecloth when the moss is wet. Be sure to protect anything valuable (or go au naturel and choose an undyed option).

What You'll Need:

- Kokedama made from sheet moss and a mix of small plants in 2- and 4-inch (5 and 10 cm) pot sizes (see page 18). Pictured here: white and purple flowering kale, white Calandiva flaming Katy, maidenhair ferns, white nerve plants, China doll plants

- Cork bark (or the bark from a few pieces of firewood)

- Candle adhesive dots (optional)

- Taper candles

▷ **Party Favors:** Assigning seats at your next dinner party is a fun throwback idea that allows for easy introductions of gregarious longtime friends to shy newcomers. Reimagine the traditional place card by tucking a small name tag in the leaves of a tiny ornamental kale kokedama.

Centerpieces should be kept relatively low so that you can easily see and converse with fellow diners. To test this, put your elbow on the table next to the centerpiece, raise your hand, and ensure that your fingers fall below the dense area of the arrangement.

GARDEN PARTY

Head out to your local garden center and pick up various grasses, roses, and succulents (echeverias and frost-tolerant houseleeks are pictured here) and place them in terra-cotta pots for an indoor-outdoor living centerpiece. Choose one primary hue and use it to tie together all your plants and accessories. Here green foliage is accented with a pale pink that shows up in the rose blooms, the underside of the creeping saxifrage, the subtle tint of the succulent rosettes, and the warm glow of a 'Red Rooster' carex grass. Include some herbs in your arrangement (like this thyme) and you can grab a bit right off the centerpiece to add to your meal—yum! Once the festivities are over, put the arrangements in a bright window or on the patio, give them to your guests, or take them apart and plant them in your garden.

Embrace the Now: These planters are jam-packed—there's no room for growth here. We're not in garden design mode, so there's no need to plan for the mature size of the plant. Make them look pretty *today*, not in a month, a year, or a season.

AN EDIBLE ARRANGEMENT

Tuck a tiny sweet bay laurel into a simple ceramic cup (this one is from Heath Ceramics), and you're well on your way to a centerpiece. Stick a few sprigs of fresh-cut rosemary in a bud vase and toss some vibrant citrus in a cereal bowl (keep a few leaves on to make it a bit more natural), and voilà—a fragrant, elegant, tasty tablescape! The minimalist vessels help unify the look.

Bay trees (*Laurus nobilis*) need bright light and moisture. They can grow up to 30 feet (9 m) tall outdoors, but this tiny plant (in a 4-inch/10 cm pot) makes for a lovely indoor starter. Take the bay from table to plate by plucking leaves from the stem, placing them on a baking sheet, and heating in the oven at a low temperature (175°F/79°C) for about an hour, until thoroughly dried. They'll last a year or more in an airtight container. You can also pluck them off the plant and immediately freeze them.

Opulent Accents: The bowl's gold hue connects the centerpiece to the other decor in this dining nook, including the wall mirror, light fixture, and pillows.

A TABLETOP JEWEL BOX

If you have a smallish table, or one that is frequently commandeered for not only the dinner rush but also rainy-day art projects and late-night homework sessions, you may not have a lot of space for additional decor. But even a *touch* of green will liven up your space. Just choose a planting that takes up a small footprint, with a low pot that is tumbleproof! This grouping of exquisite yet easy-care plants combines an angular 'Black Mystic' earth star with the fluffy flowers of the cooperi crassula and a bright Ruby Blush echeveria for a dynamic push-pull of color and texture. The solid greens of the emerald ripple peperomia, 'ihi, and soft gray echeveria serve as a unifying backdrop.

ABOVE IT ALL

For an unobtrusive yet striking centerpiece, consider the space over your head! Two of the designs below pair plants with a hanging lighting fixture, providing cozy ambience around the table.

3

1. Planted Pendant

Haworthia, a few different species of rhipsalis, rat's tail cactus, and a pickle plant make perfect companions in this high-style light fixture–as-planter by Object/Interface. Since the bulb lights the table below, not the plants above, make sure these sun-lovers get some natural light.

2. Hanging Terrarium

For another double-duty design, check out this light terrarium by Lightovo. A sweet hanging home for this moody, wild grouping, the fixture lights both the table below *and* its plant occupants. Here a rex begonia, a Sprengeri fern, and arrowhead plants were wrapped together in moss, kokedama-style (see page 18), then inserted moss-ball first into the terrarium. A single plant in a tiny pot would look nice, too. Gently water with a turkey baster or watering can with a narrow spout to avoid a pool of water in the bottom of the glass.

3. Wreath Chandelier

Turn a wreath on its side for a wild take on a traditional dining room chandelier. The wreath pictured here is hung from a three-pronged device from Terrain, but a wreath form outfitted with three wires and a hook will produce a similar look. If you're feeling crafty, gather cut greens to make your own wreath. Choose woody shrubs (such as the heavenly bamboo, bittersweet, eucalyptus, and magnolia shown here) as your foundation—they'll dry much better than lush tropicals. Add in cut protea and banksia, plus a few stems of airy grasses for flair. Finally, tuck in air plants galore (remove for a good soak once a week or so).

HIGHLIGHT THE BACKDROP

Different wall colors (and patterns) call for different colors, shapes, and styles of plant and vases to complement them. The correct pairing will enhance how the wall *and* the plant look. Mix and match to find the right combination for your space. Here are four examples to get you started.

Color Blocking

Embrace a bright wall color by carrying the hue through your planting. Here the peachy pink wall color gets picked up in the portrait and the extra-large *Tillandsia superinsignis* air plant (right), while begonia leaves in a vase (left) feature a darker tone of pink that's almost black. The green undertones in the air plant tie in to the other strong color in the room: the dusty green on the sideboard.

Repeating Patterns

Complement, don't overpower, an intricate wallpaper. The simple draping shape of the ZZ plant subtly echoes the fern pattern of this Erica Tanov wallpaper (an actual fern would have been too literal here), while its gold vase ties in with the gold-painted leaves.

Jewel Tones

Our perception of a color changes based on what it is next to. This same green wall would look different with a dark purple plant in front of it than it does against the green fatshedera shown here. The yellow trim of its variegated leaves makes the plant pop against the wall, and its pattern adds needed interest (otherwise, this green-on-green look would be too much of the same).

Pattern Mixing

Don't be afraid to break the rules: sometimes a mishmash of colors, textures, and patterns sparks curiosity and creates splendor. Here the bold patterned leaves of the peacock plant, coleus, and rex begonia are a lively backdrop for the romantic flowers of the hellebore, while the wispy asparagus ferns and creeping wire vines keep this arrangement loose and wild. The deep greens, silvers, blues, and purples hold it all together, and the orange bowl makes it pop against the checkered wallpaper.

BEDROOM

W e spend a third of our lives in bed, so our sleeping spaces should be as appealing and comforting as possible. This chapter focuses on the ways plants can help us achieve this. Amazingly, just one plant can make your bedroom air a bit fresher. You'll also discover plants that help mitigate noise and others that respond to light in a surprising and delightful way. When you're in bed, it's lovely to look out on a beautiful array of plants and connect with the calming and restorative effects of nature.

AIR PURIFIERS

Though we all know that plants take in carbon dioxide and release oxygen, they do so much more! Plants fully clean our air, removing the volatile organic compounds (VOCs) found in and released by carpets, cleaning supplies, and paint. In 1989, NASA funded research to discover the best plants for air filtration; it is still considered one of the most comprehensive studies of its kind. Here are just a few of the top contenders.

Snake Plant

The sword-like leaves of the snake plant, or mother-in-law's tongue, offer up more than a striking architectural presence. Unlike other plants, which release carbon dioxide at night, the snake plant continues to produce oxygen and absorb toxins all night long. Shown here is the 'Singer's Silver' cultivar, which tolerates low light levels and sparse watering; any *Sansevieria trifasciata* will have a similar air-cleaning effect (see page 85).

Chrysanthemum

Though temporary bloomers, *Chrysanthemum* spp., or mums, are an ideal choice for adding a splash of color to the bedroom. Don't be fooled by their soft facade: these blooming beauties are also a top pick for removing pollutants from the air while you sleep. Keep them in a cool, bright location with consistently moist soil for flowers that last up to six weeks.

Gerbera Daisy

Members of the sunflower family, gerbera daisies (*Gerbera* × hybrid) offer robust stems, sturdy leaves, and an extensive color palette. Gerberas have proven to be extremely efficient at removing chemical vapors indoors. Keep them in a cool spot with a little morning sun for several weeks of blossoms. Their soil should remain moist to the touch.

English Ivy

An easygoing bedroom companion, English ivy (*Hedera helix*) is fairly tolerant of low light. The miniature variety 'Jubilee' pictured here is but one of many varieties to choose from, all of which can tumble down bedside tables or climb up structures to create a living curtain. They have been proven to reduce allergens and indoor mold counts.

A JUNGLE HIDEAWAY

This cozy bedroom features more than a dozen plants in a pleasing assortment of forms and textures: airy, upright, sprawling, glossy. The secret to designing a full space like this one, which feels comfortable and intimate rather than crowded and claustrophobic, is to create "zones" within the room and make sure each grouping has a mix of sizes and shapes to mimic what happens in nature. Here are a few more tips.

Take it one step at a time. Let your collection grow slowly. A nightstand topped with an assemblage of plants will offer a wilder, fuller feel than the same few plants scattered around the room.

Aim high. In a real jungle, plants appear at every level, including above your head. So add a floor plant that is reaching for the ceiling (and let it drape slightly, like a canopy over the bed). You can create a similar effect with hanging planters: hang several at different heights to create a living canopy.

Add a focal point. Keep the design interesting yet restful on the eye by opting mostly for simple, soft shapes in a harmonious green color theme. But be sure to incorporate a couple of plants that stand out from the crowd due to their eye-catching color or shape. Thanks to its unusual curved trunk and huge odd-shaped leaves, the snowflake aralia (right) really holds its own, even in a busy crowd.

Clear the way. Once you get bitten by the plant bug, it might be hard to rein yourself in. But remember to keep a path wide enough to negotiate comfortably. This will protect those delicate leafy friends and save you the struggle of navigating an obstacle course each time you cross the room.

For a complete list of plants featured in this room, turn to page 272.

A BRIGHT AND SUNNY SPACE

It's easy to think of the green of foliage as a "neutral" tone, but don't forget that it can be employed as a pop of color in your space. This vibrant bedroom balances three equally strong, happy hues: sunny yellow pillows, an azure blue comforter, and the emerald green of the tiny spike moss (left) and tall snake plants (right). The textural art pieces, intricate wooden accents, and patterned pillows are offset by the relative simplicity of the flanking plants.

PLANT PALETTES

When choosing your next plants, be sure to think about the *color* of their foliage as well as their size, shape, and care requirements. Green stands in the middle of the color wheel, so it can register to our eye as a warm or a cool color. To "cool down" a hot room, add a gray-green foliaged plant such as a blue star fern. Conversely, a bright neon golden pothos and a cheery pink gerbera daisy will warm up a dim room that needs some oomph!

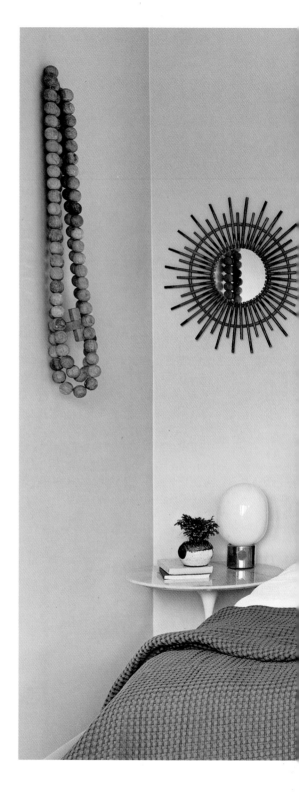

A MINIMALIST OASIS

Thanks to the exceptional large bay window, little is needed in this bedroom in the way of decoration. For a clean and calm look, you can't beat a simple white-and-green palette. Though the vining 'Jade' pothos plant opposite adds a bit of color and interest, casting a green hue as sunlight filters through its leaves, consider the planting options below if you're in search of some privacy.

Screen from Above: To create living curtains, insert a row of hooks along the ceiling and hang plants from them (for a utilitarian look, simply keep your plants in the plastic hanging grow pots they are sold in), or install a shelf just above the window and let full, draping specimens like this creeping ficus hang from it.

Screen from Below: Add privacy from below by lining up a row of tall specimens like these wide-leaved snake plants. If they need a boost, use a box, books, or a plant stand.

SLEEP LIKE A BABY

Plants are nature's sound machines: they alleviate sound pollution by reflecting, diffracting, and absorbing noise. They can soak up as much sound as a carpet! Here are a few ways to use plants to get a good night's sleep.

Go big. If you have the space, opt for a floor plant. The foliage of this 'Limelight' dracaena (in the foreground) will dampen sound, and so will its large pot and the soil in it. Though the croton (far back corner) is not a tall floor plant, its large leaves are extra-absorbent.

Stick 'em in a corner. Grouping plants together will maximize their soundproofing power. If you place your collection in a corner, noise coming from two different directions will be absorbed—a double whammy for sound reduction.

Create layers. Here, the plants are placed at varying heights: a mistletoe fig "creeps" across the floor with the dracaena and a croton on either side, and a goldfish plant and a tiny *Tillandsia ionantha* air plant on the table. You could even hang plants from the ceiling to complete the barrier against unwanted sound.

NIGHT MOVES

Believe it or not, some plants turn in for the night, too. This sleeping movement, called nyctinasty, occurs in response to darkness. Once the light levels drop, the leaves close up for the night. As the sun rises, you will see the plant "stir" from its slumbering state as its leaves stretch out to collect energy. The sensitive plant pictured here closes at night and also reacts to the slightest touch (a response called seismonasty, a defense against predators), which is why it's also commonly referred to as the touch-me-not plant. Oxalis (page 62) and prayer plant (page 77) are two more movers and shakers; keep these plants near your bedside, and you'll enjoy the rhythm of the earth's rotation together.

Open: The sensitive plant likes plenty of direct light, so it's a lively addition to a sunny room. Allow its soil to dry out a bit in between watering. It's a slightly fussy houseguest, but when treated right, it is a fast grower; prune it back to keep its mounding habit (as shown here) or it will become tall and lanky.

Closed: This plant doesn't take more than a second to respond to a poke. Its proper botanical name, *Mimosa pudica*, aptly warns of this collapse: *pudica* is Latin for bashful. Once given peace and quiet and some sunlight, it gently opens its leaves once again.

ONE DRESSER, FOUR WAYS

Turn your dresser into a vignette that celebrates your personal style. Choose easy-care plants like the ones featured here to create ambience without adding to your busy schedule.

1. Urban Bohemian

Introduce a laid-back feel by softening bold features, like this large mirror, with a vine or other climbing greenery. Here a grape ivy was attached to the mirror's frame using clear 3M hooks (which are discreet and removable).

2. Feminine Glamour

Combine softly textural plants—like the delicate beading of string of pearls (above) and the voluminous tousles of 'N'Joy' pothos (below)—with statement-making metallic accents to create an elegant space perfect for pampering and indulgence.

3. Sleek Contemporary

Monochromatic colors and subtle patterns create layers of
interest without being overwhelming. Here, the sophisticated
metallic vase mimics the shape of the mirror frame, and
the unusual, architectural 'Ming Thing' cactus within sparks
interest.

4. Natural Beauty

The vibe here is Scandinavia meets Joshua Tree. Both the
plant and the accessories are monotone, so varying textures
are key to adding interest: the woven basket against the
painted ceramic planter and the soft furry leaves of the
'Chocolate Soldier' panda plant.

TALL, DARK, AND HANDSOME

Trick your eye and create a space that feels big on green but has a small footprint. If you're tight on space, these strategies will help you squeeze in more plants without taking up valuable real estate.

3

1. Pack It In

If you want to add a whole lot of plants into a narrow space, fill a slim-line vase with a smorgasbord of sansevierias. The standard snake plant is included here, as well as more interesting varieties of sansevieria with fabulous names such as shark's fin, bird's nest, starfish, and 'Superclone'! Just like a box of assorted chocolates, it's bound to draw you in and keep you coming back for more.

2. Give It a Boost

Make a small or medium plant pull the weight of a floor plant, but in half the space, with a plant stand. This one is only 7 inches (18 cm) wide and snugly fits a plant's vase (or one can be set on top with the addition of a plate). Go even taller by choosing a vertical specimen like a snake plant or, if you have a smidgen more room to spare, add a draping plant like this rex begonia vine.

3. Train It

Variegated fatshedera (pictured here) and other climbing vines can get unruly, but tightly prune and secure the vines to a trellis with twist ties or twine (a technique called espaliering) to keep them contained and almost flat against the surface.

KID'S
ROOM

T here are a lot of reasons to have plants in a kid's room. They are fun to look at, obviously, and are also a way to give kids a bit of responsibility; plus, they are natural air purifiers and sound absorbers. Involve youngsters in the process of choosing the plants for their room—it is an excellent opportunity to teach them about the wide variety of plants out there and will help ensure that they like them and want to care for them.

The most important thing to keep in mind when choosing plants for children is that not all plants are suitable for all kids of all ages. If children are young enough that they may put plants into their mouths, choose only nontoxic specimens. And varieties that can irritate the skin, like thorny cactus, should be skipped entirely or kept out of reach. Beyond that, start with plants that don't require fussy care and can hold up to a bit of handling. Soon you might have a budding gardener in the house!

TOUGH AND TOUCHABLE PLANTS

As living things that are full of personality and completely dependent on us for care, plants can truly serve as a first step in "pet" ownership! The rough-and-tumble specimens below might quell your child's demands for a pony . . . for a while.

'Frizzle Sizzle' Albuca

Albuca spiralis 'Frizzle Sizzle' is like something out of a Dr. Seuss book! With corkscrew-like leaves and springtime spikes of yellow flowers, this onion-shaped bulb is a whimsical addition to a kid's room—and its blooms have a yummy vanilla aroma to boot. The leaves curl under drier conditions, so let the soil dry out a bit between waterings and position the plant in an area of full sun. After flowering, the plant "vanishes" as the leaves disappear and the bulb becomes dormant for summer. At this point, put it outside and water it extremely sparingly until leaves reemerge in late fall.

Panda Plant

Pictured here is the panda plant (*Kalanchoe tomentosa*). Furry, paddle-like leaves tipped with rust-colored edges help the plant conserve water, making it an eye-catching and easy-care plant pet. Let it dry out between thorough waterings, and house it in an area that receives a mixture of direct and indirect sun. Panda plants are toxic to pets; as a precaution, keep them out of reach of tiny tots, too.

Haworthia

These small, speckled succulents (members of the *Haworthia* genus) have a tremendous tolerance for neglect. They require less light than other succulents, and if you drop them (or they get tossed across the room), their tough skin holds up surprisingly well. (Soil, on the other hand, might go flying—see the Elmer's glue trick on page 215.) To turn your little plant a deep red color, *gradually* transition it to a hot, bright space (and decrease watering slightly).

Braided Spear Sansevieria

A plant with a braid! This technique is applied to a regular spear sansevieria plant (*Sansevieria cylindrica*) when it is young. The stems are braided, then ties are placed at the top of the plant. New growth, although slow, is supple enough to allow you to continue the braid, rebinding the stems at the top each time. This plant does well in low-light nooks and requires a light watering when the soil gets slightly dry. Please do not allow your child to nibble on any houseplants, but especially this one, as it is toxic.

GO WILD

When choosing plants for a child's room, add a few fun elements to make a kid feel, well, like a kid. If she likes trucks, bring 'em in and fill 'em up with rough-and-tumble plants like this dracaena (side table, bottom shelf). Playful objects like the openmouthed figure on top of the side table can also be adorned—here it is spilling out baby burro's tail sedum like a four-pronged tongue. A 'Ruby Red' rubber plant set on the floor adds a pretty pop of pink without being too flashy. (Coil a big fat rope and stick it under a floor plant to protect the floor from water damage.)

Let a small triangle ficus (in the back corner) grow along with your child—it will take time, but this spindly specimen will eventually become bushy and tall and will outgrow its "booster seat" (aka plant stand). (See page 135 for a full-size specimen.)

The two pieces of plant art on the wall above the bed are as simple as can be to create. For the mounted air plant (top), first choose your waterproof backing (and add a wall hook if needed). Add a drop of hot glue to the center of the backing, let it cool for a moment, then gently push the base of the air plant onto it. Hold for a few seconds to make sure the plant is secured; leave overnight to completely dry before hanging. Mist the air plant every few days. The moss frame (below) is created in a similar fashion—remove the glass from a picture frame, then glue dyed reindeer moss (or other dried natural elements you wish to display) to the back of the frame using Elmer's glue. Allow to dry overnight before hanging. The moss used here is dried, so the only "plant care" required is to dust the display occasionally.

LIVING NIGHT-LIGHTS

Kids' rooms tend to collect clutter—baseball card collections, favorite toys, rocks and sticks from their latest outdoor adventures. That makes planters that do double duty all the more valuable! With these light-up planter solutions, no matter the size of the nightstand, your child doesn't have to choose between a bedside lamp and a bit of green.

1

2

3

1. Color Changing

This battery-operated lit planter from Flying Tiger Copenhagen switches colors to keep things fresh. Make the look even wilder by adding a spider plant bursting with offshoots.

2. Ecosystem Sphere

These fully enclosed miniature worlds, called EcoSpheres and available at Eco-Sphere.com, contain tiny shrimp, marbling strands of algae, and microorganisms that coexist in a harmonious composition of flora and fauna. Set a sphere atop an LED stand and bask in the glow while your child watches the shrimp dance their way around the aquatic theater, dining on algae. Below, a sweet oblong planter holds an air-purifying (but toxic) ivy.

3. Tiny Terrarium

Meant to be placed in the mouth of a wine bottle, this bottle light stopper from Bed Bath & Beyond makes the sweetest lit terrarium. Create the miniature plantscape with tweezers and a steady hand, add a tiny bit of moss, and stop the top with the light stopper (which is rechargeable via a USB cable). On the shelf below, two toy trucks carry loads of succulents.

A "GROW AND LEARN" PLAYROOM

When we interact with plants from an early age, we learn to appreciate nature and are inspired to spend more time alongside it. And there is so much more youngsters can gain from early exposure to plants! Even the most low-maintenance plant requires watering and a bit of monitoring to make sure it's healthy and thriving. When caring for plants, kids will actually *see* the benefits of nurturing, in the form of new growth, blooms, and offshoots. As a bonus, while they're waiting for new shoots to grow into sturdy stalks or seasonal flowers to appear in all their colorful glory, their green friends will teach them the value of patience. Of course, plants can be a gentle introduction to the concept that every living thing undergoes cycles of growth, decay, and regeneration (particularly if you choose a plant that's dormant for part of the year, like the 'Frizzle Sizzle' albuca—see page 206).

Given all these benefits, aren't you inspired to create a mini jungle for your little ones? Turn the page to learn more about the kid-friendly ways plants appear in the playroom pictured here.

KID-FRIENDLY DISPLAYS

Just like the plants themselves, the ways you display greenery in your child's room should be fun, colorful, and durable. Here are a few ideas.

Get into the Swing

Hanging is a great option if a kid wants a plant that's delicate or otherwise not suited for handling. This 'Little Darling' begonia planted on a tire swing (which is meant as a bird feeder) is safe, out of the way, and adorable. Hang from a retractable hanging plant device (available from plant nurseries) for easy adult access.

Lead the Way

Attach some colorful jumbo hooks to the walls (these are from Flying Tiger Copenhagen) and train trailing plants (like these pothos) to wander and crawl up the wall using the hooks for support. If you've got wee ones, choose a nontoxic vine like a Madagascar jasmine, as the pothos isn't safe to ingest.

An Unconventional "Vessel"

Who says plants have to live in a pot? This little sailboat has a small carved-out section perfect for two tiny haworthia plants. For a no-mess planting, top with gravel and a fine layer of a 50-50 Elmer's glue–water mixture, and let cure for twenty-four hours. This will create a firm but permeable layer that can be watered with a dropper or spoonful of water every week or two (depending on your climate). With a firm top and stationary plants, the ship and its two passengers become almost indestructible.

A Mason Jar Terrarium

Nerve plants love humidity. Rather than buy a fancy (and delicate!) terrarium to house it, simply raid your kitchen for a mason jar. Take a tiny nerve plant or fern, uproot it, add some moss around the roots, set the plant on the lid, and gently feed it into the upside-down jar. Screw on the lid, and the terrarium is complete. Keep it out of direct sun or else the plant will burn. Bonus: this planter will self-water—set it and forget it!

GOOD EARTH

Working in the garden makes us feel good—and there's science to back up the restorative benefits of getting our hands dirty. Soil contains the harmless bacteria *Mycobacterium vaccae*, which stimulates serotonin production when breathed in, relaxing us and boosting our mood! Below are two easy "science experiments" to get your budding gardeners started.

A Test-Tube Garden

This is a kid-friendly kit (called the Root Viewer), but lab-style test tubes will work just fine. Fill containers three-quarters of the way full with moist potting mix. Next, sprinkle a few carrot seeds into each vessel and cover with about ¼ inch (6 mm) of soil. Place in a bright location, and as the seeds germinate, ensure that your child waters the plant regularly to keep the soil moist but not wet. Your kid will marvel as the seed germinates and the carrot body forms. Encourage youngsters to pull out a magnifying glass to take a closer look as the seedling develops into a carrot.

Grow-Your-Own Wheatgrass

Pictured here is the Creativity for Kids Grow 'n Glow Terrarium, but you can just as easily upcycle an old glass jar to create this mini vegetable garden. Add potting mix, colored sand, and rocks, in decorative layers (be sure the top layer is soil), then sprinkle wheatgrass seeds on the surface along with a dusting of potting mix and watch the grass grow. Water lightly with a sprinkle-spout watering can, which mimics a gentle rainfall. The cool part for your child will be watching the grass shoot out the top of the jar even as the fast-forming roots drive downward. Snip off a blade of grass and taste.

A WALL-MOUNTED WATER GARDEN

For an easy, out-of-reach option, add a miniature aquarium to your kid's wall. This plastic "bubble bowl" with a flat back is sold as a fishbowl. For the simplest setup, just add a layer of aquarium sand (which is specially formulated not to cloud or dirty the water) and a single aquatic plant. The anubias plant used here is often sold like this, attached to a rock with fishing line. The leaves of this plant can be submerged or allowed to peek out of the water—but don't bury their roots. Change the water regularly so that algae doesn't form: gently let faucet water flush (fill and let spill until clear) to clean the vessel. If you have a large enough bubble bowl, fish or aquatic snails are most welcome here (their poop will fertilize the plant!), but be sure to follow proper pet care instructions.

AQUATIC PLANTS

There's something enchanting about life submerged in an aquamarine glow. Fully aquatic plants (which live entirely underwater) and amphibious plants (which live both aboveground and underwater) make for exciting and unexpected houseplants. Many aquatic plants can be picked up at specialist aquarium stores or major pet stores. For fully aquatic plants, look for easy-to-care-for anubias (like the one pictured here) and parrot's-feather, which is an oxygenator and helps keep water clear and algae-free. Add layers to your aquascape using amphibious plants, such as Java fern, which gently waves above and below the surface. Mix and match plants in anything from old jam jars to vintage aquariums, or head to specialist aquatic supply stores for vessels dedicated to the job. The amount of maintenance your aquatic garden requires will depend on how complex your collection is. In general, once a week plan to change 50 percent of the water, clean the inside of the glass, and trim any browning leaves.

BATHROOM

Yes, a bathroom is a necessity, but it can also be a place for relaxation, comfort, and pleasure (bubble bath!). Plants are wonderful enhancements in this space—and luckily, bathrooms are welcoming places for greenery. They tend to have decent heat and humidity, which some plants require, and, like the kitchen, bathrooms typically offer water- and stain-resistant surfaces. Plus, it's the easiest room in your home in which to water your plants. Use the showerhead to mimic rainfall to clean leaves and soak the soil—but place a screen over the drain to catch dirt, gravel, and whatnot so that it doesn't clog the pipes.

FERNS

Known as pteridomania or fern fever, fern collecting became a craze during the Victorian era, when collectors began growing hundreds of these humidity-loving specimens in their greenhouses or conservatories. You can imagine your bathroom as a mini greenhouse of sorts, with plenty of hot water creating the humid atmosphere ferns need. Here are a few favorites that work well as houseplants.

Maidenhair Fern

Often thought of as tricky to grow because of its love for humidity and moisture, the maidenhair fern (*Adiantum raddianum*) is the perfect match for a steamy shower room. Place it in an area of moderate to bright light and ensure that the soil remains moist. Try to keep it away from vents or dry air sources and avoid repotting. If you're not one to create steamy conditions while showering, see tips on constructing a more humid environment on page 24.

Lemon Button Fern

This compact cultivar, *Nephrolepis cordifolia* 'Duffii', offers up sprightly thin fronds of delicate light green leaves. Small in size (reaching about 1 foot/30 cm), it is one of the easiest ferns to grow. Simply keep it in a bright yet indirectly lit spot—the sill of a frosted bathroom window is ideal.

Curly Bird's Nest Fern

Bring a tropical feel to your bathroom with the vivid, upright rosette of the aptly named curly bird's nest fern (*Asplenium nidus*). Happiest in a place with moderate to bright light and moderate moisture, it is tolerant of periods of lower light and drier conditions. New foliage spirals out from a furry central crown, thought to resemble a bird's nest (older fronds gradually turn brown and can be snipped off). Keep its broad leaves shiny by occasionally wiping them with a damp cloth.

East Indian Holly Fern

A favorite of many gardeners due to its striking striped foliage and easy attitude, the East Indian holly fern (*Arachniodes simplicior* 'Variegata') brings its woodland charm indoors, too. It is best suited to moderate to low light and consistently moist soil. Its arching, fan-like fronds can extend up to 2 feet (61 cm). Try cutting a few and tucking them into floral arrangements to add earthiness and volume.

A FERN-FILLED VANITY

If you picture ferns as old-fashioned, think again! Add some flair by pairing these timeless stunners with unique vessels. On the countertop, a vintage pedestal shows off the fullness of a lemon button fern (right), while a halved coconut shell holds a staghorn fern (left). The oversize mother fern on the floor lives in a handmade ceramic pot set on a lazy Susan to allow for weekly rotation to promote all-around even growth. Prune the outer dangling fronds for a more upright look (see the unpruned Boston fern on page 39 for the contrast). Ferns do best with humidity, so keep the soil evenly moist (not soggy), and increase ambient humidity levels by placing plants on gravel trays (see page 24). Allow ferns to bathe in bright to moderate light, but steer away from scorching direct sun, and protect the more delicate lacy varieties like mother fern from cold drafts.

Give the 'Old Spice'
pelargonium leaves
a squeeze to release
their nutty scent.

SOAK UP THE SUN

A sunny corner of the bathroom is freshened by a palette of minty green. This arrangement is a lesson in the importance of layering for scale and interest. If all of these plants were at the same height as the tub, it would make for a one-note display, and the tub would overpower the space. Instead, each plant is on its own level. The hanging succulent string of bananas draws the eye upward, but its slim, tidy silhouette keeps it from dominating the view. The naked feltleaf kalanchoe was placed in a footed planter and further elevated on a stool, and the wheeled planter features a tall pencil cactus and the lower, denser foliage of silver plectranthus. Even the tiny nutmeg-scented 'Old Spice' pelargonium is given a boost by an overturned woven basket. Thanks to this layered approach, the tub doesn't feel outsize, and the whole vignette is visually appealing. This eclectic collection likes bright light, so open the window and let the sun shine in.

THE LANGUAGE OF LEAVES

By looking at specific characteristics of a plant's leaf, you gather clues as to what light it needs to survive. Darker shades of green and larger leaf structures suggest that a plant has adapted to low-light conditions (because large surface areas and dark colors maximize light absorption). Plants with hints of teal and gray-green hues, as well as leaves that are smaller, narrower, or more complex in shape, have evolved to tolerate bright and direct light—keep them in those sunny window spots. Fuzzy and waxy surfaces contain protective layers that help screen out sun; such plants can often take a lot of light, too.

A LOW-LIGHT "TUBSCAPE"

When filling a space with loads of plants, think of your room as an indoor jungle. In the wild, some plants reach to the light of the sky, while midsize specimens thrive under the shade of a tree. Still other plants grow low to the ground, drinking up the dappled light. So when you approach your room design, consider these three planes: the space overhead, at eye level, and on the ground. If you include plants on all three levels, the space will feel more like a natural environment—you'll have to look up, down, and around to catch it all! Here's the breakdown in this space.

Overhead: Hanging plants like the spider plant (upper right) and tall floor plants like the Madagascar dragon tree (far left) not only envelop the scene in a canopy of green but also provide dramatic scale.

Eye Level: Eye level is our most common vantage point, and plants in this zone will deliver instant impact whenever we walk into a room. The snake plant (center) and monstera (right) work particularly well at this level because their bold-shaped leaves provide interest when viewed from the side.

Ground Level: Plants placed on the ground or at lower levels will frequently be seen from above. The bird's nest sansevieria shown in the gold vase here is fairly plain when viewed from the side, but glance down while entering the bathtub and you'll appreciate its charming rosette.

For a complete list of plants featured in this room, turn to page 272.

REPURPOSED ACCESSORIES

Use tiny utilitarian containers in unexpected ways to turn pint-size spaces into impressive plant displays.

At the Sink

Kokedama, a Japanese art form that translates as "moss balls," comes in many forms. (Turn to page 18 to learn how to make one.) This 'Jeanette' dwarf English ivy kokedama is perfectly suited to the bathroom sink—set on a soap dish, it's a snap to care for: simply soak in the filled sink for twenty minutes, remove, gently squeeze out excess water, and return the ball to the soap dish to finish draining. Regular misting will keep the moss looking vibrant, too.

In a Soap Dish

The corner soap dishes that come with suction-cup backs make perfect niches for air plants like these *Tillandsia stricta* 'Houston Dark Pink' and Spanish moss. After a shower, be sure to shake off excess water so that it doesn't pool in the dish and rot the moss.

On the Mirror

This tiny suction-cup holder meant to corral shaving razors (a hardware store find!) works perfectly for plant cuttings. Tropical vine-like plants such as philodendrons and pothos take well to rooting in water—just change the water occasionally and watch these babies grow. When the roots get too long, plant the cuttings in soil and replace with some fresh cuts. See page 30 for more on propagating plants. On the counter below, a small cup (part of a vanity accessories set) was repurposed as a pot for a little succulent.

From the Towel Rack

This window box is meant to hang on an outdoor railing, but why not hang it on your towel rack instead? Here it is filled with four types of bromeliads (from left to right): earth star, guzmania, vriesea, and 'Hallelujah'. Bromeliads drink from their rosettes, so water from above, allowing a tiny pool to gather in each cup. Be sure your towel rack is mounted securely and can take the weight of the plants, then set the grow pots inside (eliminating the extra weight of soil packed between plants).

A GREEN APOTHECARY

Medicinal herbs have been used for centuries, by ancient Egyptians and Babylonians, medieval monks, and even modern-day physicians. Many of the findings from early herbalists became milestones in Western medicine as we're familiar with it today. There's something particularly rewarding about growing plants with a practical use, especially when they provide you with not only a stylish medicine cabinet but also the comfort of knowing a homegrown first-aid kit is always on hand. Whether you're going to use the scent to relax or the gel to soothe, all of these plants are helpful additions to a sunny bathroom.

A NATURAL COLD REMEDY

Homes can become warm, dry, and stuffy in winter. Plants release oxygen and raise the humidity level, which can reduce the chance of contracting a cold. Don't worry; your plant-filled bath won't turn into a steam room, even if you've created your own private jungle.

1. **Aloe:** This succulent (*Aloe vera*) is durable, easy to grow, and quick to multiply. When the leaves are cut, they release a gel that soothes burns and promotes healing—and can be added to homemade beauty products like face washes and hydrating masks.

2. **Rosemary:** This herb has uses that extend far beyond culinary creations. Cut off a piece or two, put in hot water, and breathe in the scent for a quick pick-me-up and to help open up a stuffed nose during allergy or cold season. Rosemary (*Rosmarinus officinalis*) comes in both upright and draping varieties. To re-create this bonsai-style form, pick out a draping variety in a 4-inch (10 cm) grow pot and prune to shape.

3. **Coconut Palm:** If planted in the ground outside in a warm climate, this palm (*Cocos nucifera*) will grant you coconuts in about five years (it will also grow up to 50 feet/15 m tall). You can bring it indoors and plant it in a small pot to keep it manageably small, but then you're not likely to see fruit. Even if you can't drink the milk and reap the medicinal benefits, it should soothe the soul with its tropical innuendoes.

4. **Lavender:** This workhorse (*Lavandula* spp.) acts as an air purifier, and its aroma reduces anxiety. Release its fragrance by simply rubbing the flowers or leaves. Lavender dries extremely well, too—collect the petals into a small sachet to tuck under your pillow or place in your drawers to subtly scent your clothes or sheets.

A WALL OF EPIPHYTES

A sunlit shower is the perfect host to a collection of mounted epiphytes—each plant gets sprinkled with water and can enjoy high humidity and bright light. Ready-made mounted plants are available from garden centers and online crafters, but they're easy to make on your own. Simply follow the steps below.

1. Rest the plant horizontally on a piece of cork and wrap fishing line around the two to secure.

2. Add moss or colored twine if you wish, for further decoration.

3. Attach to a bathroom wall with adhesive hooks.

What You'll Need:

- 1 epiphytic plant (a plant that grows on other plants, rather than in soil); pictured here are a Jenkins's dendrobium orchid (top) and a *Tillandsia brachycaulos × concolor* air plant (center)

- Cork bark

- Fishing wire

- Moss or colored twine (optional)

- Waterproof, heavy-weight-bearing adhesive hooks

▷ **A Potted Pair:** Below the mounted dendrobium orchid and air plant is a handmade wall-hanging orchid pot. This one has a flat back and a carved design that allow for easy hanging, air circulation, and drainage, perfect for an upright miniature orchid and dangling pink lipstick plant (*Aeschynanthus* 'Thai Pink').

CLEANING YOUR PLANTS

Too much dust on a plant's leaves will clog its respiration "pores," so clean leaves periodically with a duster, small paintbrush, damp soft cloth, or mister, or take your plant for a quick dip under the showerhead or the spray nozzle of the sink (support the leaves with your hand as you clean). A paintbrush or cloth is best for cleaning furry or prickly plants.

HOME
OFFICE

The benefits of green things is a topic that's hot in the press and backed by science, too. And now, researchers from the United Kingdom, the Netherlands, and Australia suggest that we make fewer mistakes, have more positive feelings, and can be more productive when surrounded by even a few houseplants in the office. After studying the subject for a decade, the team concluded that folks working in an office landscaped with plants can see a 15 percent increase in productivity compared to those working in stark office environments. The following pages offer plenty of efficiency-boosting specimens. And because a room often filled with paper and expensive technology may not be conducive to lots of potting soil and water, there are plenty of mess-free options here as well.

AIR PLANTS

Unlike the more familiar terrestrial plants that grow in the ground, most air plants (botanically in the genus *Tillandsia*) are epiphytes, meaning they grow on the trunks, stems, and branches of other plants. Because they require no soil, they are the perfect choice for the office (electronics and wet soil don't mix!). Here are dirt-defying choices—see display ideas on pages 246–247.

Tillandsia tectorum

The snowflake-like appearance of this air plant is due to its feathery trichomes, which absorb moisture and nutrients from the air and help the plant survive long dry spells. Although it can withstand long periods without water and doesn't need a full-on dunk, this air plant enjoys a misting now and again. It's slow growing, meaning it's not the cheapest option, but it is sure to stay looking sweet even if you're buried in work and occasionally forget to care for it.

Tillandsia xerographica

This statement maker's tough silvery leaves blush with a rosy pigment. Place it in bright light and mist occasionally or dunk it in a water bath once a month. The large center of this species is prone to collecting water; shake it after soaking so that it doesn't develop crown rot. These slow growers can be found in diameters of just a few inches (7 cm) to almost a foot across and with leaves that swirl and stretch downward. For a larger, more mature specimen, see page 35.

Tillandsia stricta 'Houston Dark Pink'

The silver and light green leaves of the 'Houston Dark Pink' cultivar give way to a pink bract that eventually unveils a lavender-colored flower. When it begins to bloom, its stem-like flower inflorescence turns a vivid pink. Once the flowers subside, watch for one to three "pups" developing off the parent plant. You can leave the pups attached to form clumps of plants to hang alongside your desk lamp. Or gently remove the pups to create new single specimens (see page 30).

Tillandsia ionantha

One of the most affordable and common air plants available, *Tillandsia ionantha* is compact in size, making it great for scattering about the home or office. *Ionantha* means "violet flower," so look for an emerging bud when you purchase your plant, which signals a forthcoming bloom. There are numerous varieties of *T. ionantha*, all with slight coloration on their green base. Place them in an area of filtered bright light and mist them frequently.

TO THE MAX

For a desk that's bursting with inspiration, create a lush display filled with plants of all sizes, as well as tchotchkes, memorabilia, favorite books, and quirky vases. The central shelves of this flexible shelving system were aligned to help "center" and lend a sense of order to this busy design. For interest, though, the top shelves were staggered—and the highest shelf is much deeper than those below it. Books were used to add height (and serve as mini plant stands) and were stacked both horizontally and vertically to help break up the lines of the design.

If you're creating a shelving unit with a bounty of plants, be sure to add some with distinctive personalities, like the twirls of 'Frizzle Sizzle' albuca, tiny fruits on the mistletoe fig, or the curved trunk of a bonsai ficus. Draping plants are great for breaking up the lines in the shelves; try the kangaroo ivy, glory bower, or prayer plant. Then fill in with solid green foliage with some visual interest, like the coin-shaped ones of the *Pilea peperomioides* and the ear-shaped leaves of the large 'Congo' philodendron. *For a complete list of plants featured in this room, turn to page 272.*

Turn Cut Flowers into Plants: This colorful foliage from a ti plant was originally meant for a cut floral arrangement. Give it a new life as a houseplant by snipping off a few stems and placing them in water in a somewhat bright area. (Use a clear glass vessel so you can tell if the water gets cloudy and needs changing, and so that you can watch the roots grow.) Transfer to a potting mix after roots form. Once planted, place in an area of medium to bright light. Allow the soil to dry out between waterings.

STYLE TO SPARE

Plants can add beauty and interest without overpowering a room or creating unwanted clutter. In this minimalist workspace, air plants and an echeveria are kept out of the way when hung from sculpture-like planters and the desktop foliage is relatively small and unobtrusive; the brown and blue palette of the vessels add to the calming effect. Many of the plants here do double duty—they are decorative, but they also carry symbolic meaning in the ancient Chinese tradition of feng shui.

1. **Bonsai Ficus:** Bonsai is a Japanese art form in which trees and shrubs are pruned, trained, and maintained in small, specific shapes. Those with arching forms (like the one shown here) can soften hard lines in the surrounding design and are said to bring air flow through stagnant spaces—great for getting ideas flowing. According to feng shui tradition, trees promote career growth and inspire us to "reach higher" and to put down solid roots.

2. **Haworthia and Bird's Nest Sansevieria:** Practitioners of feng shui believe that spiky plants like this haworthia (left) and sansevieria (right) are excellent for shielding us against negative energy (*sha* chi). Though small, they have mighty powers!

3. **Lucky Bamboo:** This specimen (which isn't actually a bamboo—it's related to the dracaena family) is one of the most highly regarded plants in the tradition of feng shui. A display containing three stalks is the most popular, believed to bring a harmonic balance of happiness (*fu*), long life (*soh*), and wealth (*lu*). In general, the more stalks, the greater the blessing—but shy away from a grouping of four, which is said to bring *sha* chi (negative energy) to the bearer. As a bonus, there's no messy soil needed here: set your creation in a widemouthed bowl and keep it filled with water—the roots will expand and the bamboo will continue to grow upward. (Occasionally remove the plant from the bowl, rinse the roots, and refresh the water.)

CONTROLLED NATURE

Are you attracted to the tidiness of a freshly mowed lawn? Does a precisely trimmed topiary woo you? If so, you're attracted to controlled plant design rather than wild and woolly schemes. Choose a few clean-lined plants like a braided spear sansevieria (pictured here on the desktop) to convey control and stability, and introduce natural repetition and muted colors into your setup to help make for a calm, orderly space. Here are a few tips.

Stay on the same plane. All the shelves in this desk unit are aligned, so the foundation of the design is planned and predictable.

Ground with color. The monochromatic gray-blue palette evokes the feeling of water and the sky, inducing a feeling of calm.

Follow the rule of threes. Engaging, effective, and efficient, things presented in threes are pleasing to our eyes. Here the three pots on the top row allow the human brain to create a center point and rest the eye as the two others add balance. Choose three vases and plant combinations that are similar (here they all are planted with pinstripe and rose-painted calatheas; the center one varies slightly, with an added bird's nest sansevieria).

Create a pattern. Repetition ties the look together and generally makes us feel secure. Here the connecting threads are the metallic objects and the "natural" accents. The rock in glass is an art piece by Lawrence LaBianca, the eggshell-embellished vases evoke robins' eggs, and the large pot on the floor (holding a Japanese aralia) looks like it's made of stone.

Keep it simple. Here's a novel, hands-off way to bring something intriguing into the office space: the miniature orchid on top of the file boxes here, sold as *Psygmorchis pusilla* or *Erycina pusilla*, stands just 2 inches (5 cm) tall in its enclosed environment and produces yellow blooms.

A CLEAN AND CLEAR DESKTOP

Not only are air plants mess-free, they also can be stuck in just about any out-of-the-way spot on your desktop! Below are a few ways to display them. For more on air plants, turn to page 238.

3

1. Wire It

Wrap a heavy-gauge but malleable wire around the base of your air plant (*Tillandsia brachycaulos × abdita* is shown here) and insert it into a tiny drilled hole in a block of wood to create a miniature sculpture. Remove the plant from the block to soak, or mist it.

2. Glue It

Use a glue gun or nontoxic clear, waterproof glue to attach your specimen to a paperweight, a magnet, or a little vase like this one. If using hot glue, let it dry for a moment before applying the plant so you don't burn it. Hold the air plant in place for a bit to stabilize it, then let the glue set before hanging.

3. Tuck It

Spanish moss or even small air plant varieties are tiny enough to tuck into a wire organizer (as shown here); you can also clip the plants to the wire with a binder clip. They are easy to remove, water, and replace.

FOUR MINIATURE LANDSCAPES

If your space doesn't have a window, build a little plant scene and daydream of the great outdoors. Give yourself a desktop reminder of that beach vacation from last year, or re-create a calming walk in the wilderness. What escape will you create?

A Sunny Desert

This small ox tongue succulent (*Gasteria limpopo*) rests in what was intended as an ashtray but now serves as the planter's coaster. Place the succulent in the bowl of the ashtray, fill the opening with cactus mix, and display in a moderate to well-lit spot. Add a thin layer of stones on top of the soil to complete the handsome display.

A Lakefront

Awaken the memories of summer with a tiny water garden made of rocks, sand, and marimo. Keep it cool and in low light (no direct or bright light, please). Flush the old water with clean cold H_2O every ten days or so. As an added benefit, according to feng shui tradition, still water is said to improve wisdom, clarity, and wealth.

A Forest Floor

This terrarium-esque vessel by Modern Sprout is made specifically for moss, but you don't need to purchase a special display: simply plop moss in a low bowl and you can almost feel the softness of green underfoot. The lid keeps the moss moist, but if its color fades from bright green to brownish, it needs additional humidity: mist or remove and give it a soak. Keep out of bright or direct light.

A Sandy Beach

Choose any clear glass vessel, pour in two tones of sand one after the other, add a wave design by puncturing one layer into another with a toothpick, and top with a tiny air plant. Every few weeks, remove the air plant and soak it, then shake off excess water, pat dry, and replace.

BUSINESS AND PLEASURE

If your desktop real estate is particularly precious, consider wall-mounted vessels. And while elsewhere you've seen how to repurpose household items as containers for your plants, here we do the reverse—leave a couple of planters empty and use them as tidy homes for office supplies!

Graphic Design

These narrow peach vases keep a low profile on your wall. If you have a dark office, use them to hold ivy (left) and a pair of spear sansevieria (right)—plants that won't take up much space and can handle low light levels and a bit of neglect. Be mindful of ivy: if you don't want it to climb and stick to your wall (and potentially cause damage to your paint), choose a different green companion.

Industrial Chic

Hang these leather-and-rope planters from hardware accessories–turned-hooks for a rugged, DIY look. The connection between these pencils and their plant companion extends beyond their yellowish hue—this sculptural specimen is commonly called a 'Sticks on Fire' pencil cactus. This vibrant plant keeps its orange coloring best in direct light.

A POP OF COLOR

These four weird and wonderful desktop plants bring a figurative breath of fresh air to your office space, especially when paired with equally vibrant vessels!

Croton

The leaves of croton plants often have a waxy shine that emphasizes their varied colors, which range from yellow and green to orange and even dark purple. Their busy leaf patterns are equally diverse—they can be spotted, veined, striped, or speckled. These eclectic attributes are the reason for the plant's other common name, Joseph's coat (in reference to the many-hued coat of biblical lore). Embrace its bold nature by giving it an equally color-saturated pot. Be warned that this houseplant is rather fussy—it likes bright light indoors, high humidity, and soil kept slightly moist.

Earth Star

This 'Pink Starlite' earth star (also called a bromeliad) will be at its most colorful if grown in bright light. It benefits from humidity, so mist often (it's a perfect fit for tidy desktop terrariums, too!). Contrast its beautiful pink leaves with an underplanting of moss. Let it tip over the side of a low vase to give yourself a lovely view while you're hard at work.

Crown of Thorns

Paired with a handsome blue vase, this exquisite bloomer is lovely to look at, though not to touch. Don't let the pretty yellow flowers of this cultivar (*Euphorbia milii* 'Dinni Yellow') fool you—this plant is aptly named, bearing sharp thorns underneath its succulent foliage. More commonly found with red or orange flowers, crown of thorns plants need direct light and dry soil. In some cultures, they are believed to confer good luck on the plant owners and their homes.

Neon Cactus

This is actually two plants in one. The top cactus (*Gymnocalycium mihanovichii* var. *friedrichii* 'Hibotan') has a mutation that causes it to lack the chlorophyll that makes plants green, thereby exposing the red, orange, or yellow color beneath; it is grafted onto another, taller cactus (usually *Hylocerus undatus*). This cupcake-liner-like vase makes the pairing extra sweet. Give it bright light, and let it dry out between waterings.

THE ANATOMY OF A BOOKSHELF

There are countless approaches when it comes to creating a good-looking bookshelf. But let's keep it simple. Here's my go-to formula: 1 airy plant + 1 draping plant + 1 structural plant. Put these three together and you've got a pleasing combination (though, of course, you can always add more, as I've done opposite). By introducing a mix of textures and forms, you are well on your way to an interesting design. Some provide a much-needed backdrop while others make the whole design sing with their eye-catching looks. Read below for more about each plant type, then turn the page to see two more stellar combinations. And because a bookshelf isn't a spot where you want to contend with unwanted water runoff, be sure to add an extra layer of protection: here, the croton is set atop pot feet (these are from Terrain, but terra-cotta ones are readily available at garden centers); cork coasters are used on the other plants on the shelf.

Airy Plants: This foliage dances in the breeze and is often highly detailed and soft to the touch (think lacy maidenhair ferns, such as the *Adiantum raddianum* 'Microphyllum' shown here on the bottom shelf).

Draping Plants: Draping plants like a spider plant or Swiss cheese vine (pictured here, top right) lead the eye with long limbs and tentacles. They're the plants that look clumsy at floor level but can add movement and soften the edge of a shelf with elegance.

Structural Plants: These provide bold shapes. They are the plants that consist of only a few "lines" and can be either rounded like this croton (far left) or more linear like this variegated song of India (center).

TWO OFFBEAT BOOKSHELF COMBOS

1. FOR THE SUNNY STUDY

Airy: Ant Plant

In nature, an ant plant (*Hydnophytum formicarum*) encourages ant colonization within the walls of its tuberous stem—in return, the plant gets natural fertilizers from ant scraps, and these creatures serve as added protection from hungry herbivores. Don't worry, though—if you bring this one home, I don't think you'll bring any ants with you! Ant plants thrive with warm temperatures, bright light, high humidity, and dry to slightly moist conditions.

Draping: Rat's Tail Cactus

The rat's tail cactus (*Disocactus flagelliformis*) features stems that can extend up to 4 feet (1.2 m), with stunning vibrant flowers appearing in spring and summer. Water it more frequently when it's in bloom and keep it in direct sun or bright light. Be careful of its tiny thorns!

Structural: Crested Milkhedge

The fan shape of this bulbous, strange character (called a cristate or crested form) is due to a mutation that changes the milkhedge's growing habit from the usual singular point to several crowded ones. This euphorbia variety (*Euphorbia nivulia* 'Crest'), like others, does best with high light and low water levels. Look for any variation of the word *monstrose* or *crested* to find a similarly quirky plant specimen.

AIRY

DRAPING

STRUCTURAL

2. FOR THE LOW-LIGHT STUDIO

Airy: Buddha's Hand Elephant Ear

The Buddha's hand elephant ear (*Alocasia cucullata*) is often seen waving in good luck around Buddhist temples in tropical areas of Asia. It needs a lot of moisture but can handle a wide range of light conditions. If you can't find it locally, try a mail-order company.

Draping: Spider Plant

Relaxed or curly (like this 'Bonnie' curly variety) . . . either way, the spider plant (*Chlorophytum comosum*) is super easy to find and to take care of. It can handle anything from bright to low light; it should be kept relatively moist—let its soil dry just a bit between waterings. For more on spider plants (and how to propagate their offshoots), see page 86.

Structural: Starfish Sansevieria

The low-maintenance starfish sansevieria (*Sansevieria cylindrica* 'Boncel') is a great choice for an office. It doesn't demand much in the way of water or light, so you can focus on work. Just remember that as with all plants, the more light you give it, the more water it will need; keep things somewhat moist, or allow to dry just slightly between showers.

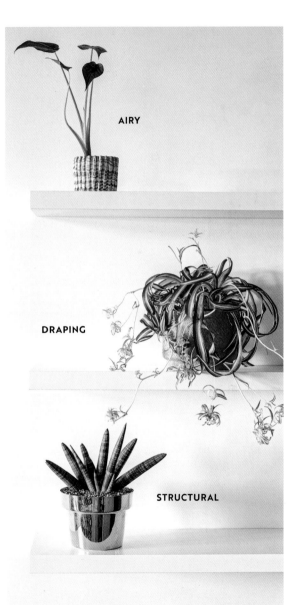

AIRY

DRAPING

STRUCTURAL

APPENDIX
COMMON AND BOTANICAL NAMES

Below is a list of the common and Latin botanical names for all of the plants featured in this book. The same plant may have multiple common names but will have only one botanical name. Botanical names can be confusing, so here's a little primer: The first part of the name is the genus, which is like a last name or family name—a large group of plants may share it. The species name, which appears second, is specific and individual to each type of plant. (Note: "spp."—which may appear at the end of a plant's Latin name—is an abbreviation of species and is used when referring to all species within a given genus.) Finally, there is sometimes a third part of the name, the variety and/or cultivar, which further defines the plant and is often used to describe color, scent, or the like. Varieties occur naturally (in the wild), while cultivars are—as their name suggests—cultivated; "cv." is used to indicate an unknown cultivar of a species.

COMMON NAME	BOTANICAL NAME
African blue basil	*Ocimum kilimandscharicum*
African violet	*Saintpaulia* cv.
air plant	*Tillandsia bergeri,* *T. brachycaulos × abdita,* *T. brachycaulos × concolor,* *T. caliginosa, T. ionantha,* *T. mooreana, T. streptophylla,* *T. superinsignis, T. tectorum,* *T. xerographica*
'Alii' ficus, 'Alii' fig	*Ficus maclellandii* 'Alii'
aloe	*Aloe vera*
alpine schefflera	*Schefflera alpina*
aluminum plant	*Pilea cadierei*
'Amate Soleil' umbrella tree	*Schefflera* 'Amate Soleil'
'Angyo Star' fatshedera	× *Fatshedera lizei* 'Angyo Star'
ant plant	*Hydnophytum formicarum*
anubias	*Anubias* spp.
aquamarine pilea	*Pilea libanensis*
Arabian coffee	*Coffea arabica*
areca palm	*Dypsis lutescens*
arrowhead plant	*Syngonium podophyllum* cv.
artillery plant	*Pilea microphylla*
asparagus fern	*Asparagus setaceus*
'Attar of Roses' pelargonium	*Pelargonium* 'Attar of Roses'
baby burro's tail	*Sedum morganianum* 'Burrito'

COMMON NAME	BOTANICAL NAME
baby rubber plant	*Peperomia obtusifolia*
banana-leaf ficus	*Ficus maclellandii* 'Alii'
begonia	*Begonia rhizomatous* cv.
Bengal fig	*Ficus benghalensis* 'Audrey'
bird's nest sansevieria	*Sansevieria trifasciata* 'Hahnii'
'Black Beauty' imperial taro	*Colocasia esculenta* 'Black Beauty'
'Black Magic' earth star	*Cryptanthus* 'Black Mystic'
blue star fern	*Phlebodium aureum*
'Bonnie' curly spider plant	*Chlorophytum comosum* 'Bonnie'
bonsai ficus	*Ficus retusa*
Boston fern, Boston swordfern	*Nephrolepis exaltata*
'Brasil' heartleaf philodendron, 'Brasil' philodendron	*Philodendron hederaceum* 'Brasil'
'Bronze Crown' air plant	*Tillandsia* 'Bronze Crown'
Buddha's hand elephant ear	*Alocasia cucullata*
bunny ears cactus	*Opuntia microdasys*
'Burgundy' rubber plant	*Ficus elastica* 'Burgundy'
burro's tail	*Sedum morganianum*
butterfly palm	*Dypsis lutescens*
caladium	*Caladium* cv.
Calandiva flaming Katy	Calandiva *Kalanchoe* *blossfeldiana*

COMMON NAME	BOTANICAL NAME
calla lily	*Zantedeschia rehmannii* hybrid
cane tree	*Dracaena* spp.
Cape primrose	*Streptocarpus* hybrid
carnosa hoya	*Hoya carnosa*
cast iron plant	*Aspidistra elatior*
Catatante orchid	*Odontocidium* Catatante 'Pacific Sun Spots'
Charmed Wine oxalis	*Oxalis triangularis* 'Jroxburwi'
chenille plant	*Acalypha hispida, A. pendula*
'China Curl' begonia	*Begonia* 'China Curl'
China doll	*Radermachera sinica*
Chinese money plant	*Pilea peperomioides*
'Chocolate Soldier' panda plant	*Kalanchoe tomentosa* 'Chocolate Soldier'
Christmas rose	*Helleborus* spp.
chrysanthemum	*Chrysanthemum* spp.
coconut palm	*Cocos nucifera*
coleus	*Coleus scutellarioides* cv.
'Colocho' pelargonium	*Pelargonium graveolens* 'Colocho'
'Congo' philodendron	*Philodendron* 'Congo'
cooperi crassula	*Crassula exilis* subsp. *cooperi*
copper spoons kalanchoe	*Kalanchoe orgyalis*
'Coppertone' sansevieria	*Sansevieria kirkii* var. *pulchra* 'Coppertone'
corn plant	*Dracaena* spp.
creeping ficus	*Ficus pumila*
creeping saxifrage	*Saxifraga stolonifera*
creeping wire vine	*Muehlenbeckia axillaris*
crested elkhorn	*Euphorbia lactea* cv. grafted to *E. neriifolia*
crested milkhedge	*Euphorbia nivulia* 'Crest'
cretan brake fern	*Pteris cretica* 'Mayii'
croton	*Codiaeum variegatum* cv.
curly bird's nest fern	*Asplenium nidus*
cymbidium orchid	*Cymbidium* spp.
dancing lady orchid	*Oncidium* spp.
Devotion echeveria	Devotion *Echeveria pulvinata*
'Dinni Yellow' crown of thorns	*Euphorbia milii* 'Dinni Yellow'
'Dorado' dracaena	*Dracaena fragrans* 'Dorado'
dwarf umbrella plant	*Schefflera arboricola*
earth star	*Cryptanthus* cv.

COMMON NAME	BOTANICAL NAME
East Indian holly fern	*Arachniodes simplicior* 'Variegata'
elephant ear	*Alocasia* spp.
emerald ripple peperomia	*Peperomia caperata*
English ivy	*Hedera helix* cv.
'Escargot' begonia	*Begonia* 'Escargot'
ewaldiana mistletoe cactus	*Rhipsalis ewaldiana*
'Fairy' begonia	*Begonia* 'Fairy'
false palm	*Dracaena* spp.
fancy-leaf zonal geranium	*Pelargonium* × *hortorum* 'Brocade Fire'
fatshedera	× *Fatshedera lizei*
'Fernwood' sansevieria	*Sansevieria* 'Fernwood'
fiddle-leaf fig	*Ficus lyrata*
'Fire' Chinese evergreen	*Aglaonema* 'Fire'
'Fireworks' begonia	*Begonia* 'Fireworks'
fishbone cactus	*Epiphyllum anguliger* cv.
flaming Katy	*Kalanchoe blossfeldiana*
flowering kale	*Brassica oleracea*
forest cactus	*Rhipsalis* spp.
foxtail palm	*Wodyetia bifurcata*
friendship plant	*Pilea involucrata*
'Frizzle Sizzle' albuca	*Albuca spiralis* 'Frizzle Sizzle'
gardenia	*Gardenia jasminoides*
gerbera daisy	*Gerbera* × hybrid
glory bower	*Clerodendrum thomsoniae*
golden ball cactus	*Notocactus leninghausii*
golden cane palm	*Dypsis lutescens*
golden pothos	*Epipremnum aureum*
golden variegated lemon thyme	*Thymus* × *citriodorus* 'Aureus'
goldfish plant	*Columnea gloriosa*
grape hyacinth	*Muscari armeniacum* cv.
grape ivy	*Cissus rhombifolia*
guzmania bromeliad	*Guzmania lingulata*
hairy-fruited wickerwork cactus	*Rhipsalis pilocarpa*
'Hallelujah' billbergia	*Billbergia* 'Hallelujah'
Hawaiian snow bush	*Breynia disticha*
haworthia	*Haworthia* spp.
heart ivy, heartleaf ivy	*Hedera helix* 'Scutifolia'
heartleaf philodendron	*Philodendron scandens*

COMMON NAME	BOTANICAL NAME
hellebore	*Helleborus* spp.
hippeastrum	*Hippeastrum* spp.
'Hope' peperomia	*Peperomia* 'Hope'
houseleek	*Sempervivum tectorum*
'Houston Dark Pink' air plant	*Tillandsia stricta* 'Houston Dark Pink'
hoya	*Hoya* spp.
hydrangea	*Hydrangea macrophylla*
'ihi	*Portulaca molokiniensis*
ivy	*Hedera helix* cv.
Jack's beanstalk	*Castanospermum australe*
'Jade' pothos	*Epipremnum aureum* 'Jade'
'Janet Craig' compacta dracaena	*Dracaena compacta* 'Janet Craig'
Japanese aralia	*Fatsia japonica*
jasmine	*Jasminum polyanthum*
Java fern	*Microsorum pteropus*
'Jeanette' dwarf English ivy	*Hedera helix* 'Jeanette'
Jenkins's dendrobium orchid	*Dendrobium jenkinsii*
Joseph's coat	*Codiaeum variegatum* cv.
'Jubilee' English ivy	*Hedera helix* 'Jubilee'
jungle cactus	*Rhipsalis* spp.
kangaroo ivy	*Cissus antarctica*
'Kent Beauty' oregano	*Origanum* 'Kent Beauty'
kentia palm	*Howea forsteriana*
'Kirigami' ornamental oregano	*Origanum* × *hybrida* 'Kirigami'
kiwi dragon tree	*Dracaena marginata*
Krimson Queen hoya	Krimson Queen *Hoya carnosa*
lady's slipper orchid	*Paphiopedilum* spp.
'Laurentii' snake plant	*Sansevieria trifasciata* 'Laurentii'
lavender	*Lavandula* spp.
lavender scallops	*Kalanchoe fedtschenkoi* cv.
lemon button fern	*Nephrolepis cordifolia* 'Duffii'
lemon cypress	*Cupressus macrocarpa* 'Goldcrest Wilma'
lemongrass	*Cymbopogon citratus*
'Lemon Lime' dracaena	*Dracaena fragrans* 'Lemon Lime'
Lenten rose	*Helleborus* spp.
'Limelight' dracaena	*Dracaena fragrans* 'Limelight'

COMMON NAME	BOTANICAL NAME
'Lisa' cane tree	*Dracaena fragrans* 'Lisa'
'Little Darling' begonia	*Begonia* 'Little Darling'
Little Phil philodendron	*Philodendron* 'PHIL01'
'Lola' echeveria	*Echeveria* 'Lola'
lucky bamboo	*Dracaena sanderiana*
Madagascar dragon tree	*Dracaena marginata*
Madagascar jasmine	*Stephanotis floribunda*
Madagascar palm	*Pachyphytum lamerei*
Magic Carousel hydrangea	Magic Carousel *Hydrangea macrophylla*
maidenhair fern	*Adiantum raddianum*
'Malaika' dracaena	*Dracaena fragrans* 'Malaika'
'Marble' baby rubber plant	*Peperomia obtusifolia* 'Marble'
marimo	*Aegagropila linnaei*
'Marisela' prayer plant	*Maranta leuconeura* 'Marisela'
metallic palm	*Chamaedorea metallica*
'Microphyllum' maidenhair fern	*Adiantum raddianum* 'Microphyllum'
milk bush	*Euphorbia tirucalli*
Ming aralia	*Polyscias fruticosa*
'Ming Thing' cactus	*Cereus* 'Ming Thing'
miniature fishtail palm	*Chamaedorea metallica*
miniature orchid	*Erycina pusilla, Psygmorchis pusilla*
miniature rose	*Rosa* hybrid
mini Hawaiian snow bush	*Breynia disticha* cv.
missionary plant	*Pilea peperomioides*
mistletoe cactus	*Rhipsalis baccifera*
mistletoe fig	*Ficus deltoidea*
monkey cups	*Nepenthes* spp.
monstera	*Monstera deliciosa*
moss ball	*Aegagropila linnaei*
mother fern	*Asplenium bulbiferum*
mother-in-law's tongue	*Sansevieria trifasciata*
moth orchid	*Phalaenopsis* spp.
mum	*Chrysanthemum* spp.
naked feltleaf kalanchoe	*Kalanchoe beharensis* var. *subnuda*
Napoleon's hat	*Kalanchoe beharensis*
'Needlepoint' dracaena	*Dracaena* 'Needlepoint'
'Needlepoint' English ivy	*Hedera helix* 'Needlepoint'

COMMON NAME	BOTANICAL NAME
neon cactus	*Gymnocalycium mihanovichii* var. *friedrichii* 'Hibotan' grafted to *Hylocerus undatus*
neon pothos	*Epipremnum aureum* 'Neon'
nerve plant	*Fittonia albivenis* Verschaffeltii Group
'N'Joy' pothos	*Epipremnum aureum* 'N'Joy'
nong noch vine	*Petraeovitex bambusetorum*
obovata hoya	*Hoya obovata*
octopus tree	*Schefflera actinophylla* 'Amate'
'Old Spice' pelargonium	*Pelargonium fragrans* 'Old Spice'
olive	*Olea europaea* cv.
oncidium orchid	*Onicidium* spp.
orange medinilla	*Medinilla scortechinii*
oregano	*Origanum vulgare*
oxalis	*Oxalis* spp.
ox tongue	*Gasteria limpopo*
paddle plant	*Kalanchoe luciae*
'Painted Lady' philodendron	*Philodendron* 'Painted Lady'
pancake plant	*Pilea peperomioides*
panda plant	*Kalanchoe tomentosa*
paperwhite	*Narcissus papyraceus*
paphiopedilum orchid	*Paphiopedilum* spp.
parallel peperomia	*Peperomia puteolata*
parlor palm	*Chamaedorea elegans*
parrot's-feather	*Myriophyllum aquaticum*
'Partita' begonia	*Begonia dregei* 'Partita'
peacock plant	*Calathea makoyana*
pencil cactus	*Euphorbia tirucalli*
'Perle von Nürnberg' echeveria	*Echeveria* 'Perle von Nürnberg'
phalaenopsis orchid	*Phalaenopsis* spp.
pickle plant	*Senecio stapeliaeformis*
piggyback plant	*Tolmiea menziesii*
pineapple	*Ananas comosus* cv.
pink lipstick plant	*Aeschynanthus* 'Thai Pink'
'Pink Starlite' earth star	*Cryptanthus* 'Pink Starlite'
pinstripe calathea	*Calathea ornata*
pitcher plant	*Sarracenia* spp.
pixie peperomia	*Peperomia orba*
poinsettia	*Euphorbia pulcherrima* cv.

COMMON NAME	BOTANICAL NAME
ponytail palm	*Beaucarnea recurvata*
prayer plant	*Maranta leuconeura*
purple waffle plant	*Hemigraphis alternata*
queen's tears	*Billbergia nutans*
rat's tail cactus	*Disocactus flagelliformis*
red prayer plant	*Maranta leuconeura*
'Red Ripple' peperomia	*Peperomia caperata* 'Red Ripple'
'Red Rooster' carex	*Carex buchananii* 'Red Rooster'
Red Velvet echeveria	Red Velvet *Echeveria pulvinata*
resurrection plant	*Selaginella lepidophylla*
rex begonia	*Begonia* Rex Cultorum Group
rex begonia vine	*Cissus discolor*
rhipsalis	*Rhipsalis* spp.
rosemary	*Rosmarinus officinalis*
rose-painted calathea	*Calathea roseopicta*
'Rosso' peperomia	*Peperomia caperata* 'Rosso'
round-leaf calathea	*Calathea orbifolia*
rubber plant	*Ficus elastica*
Ruby Blush echeveria	Ruby Blush *Echeveria pulvinata*
'Ruby' earth star	*Cryptanthus* 'Ruby'
'Ruby Red' rubber plant	*Ficus elastica* 'Ruby Red'
saber ficus	*Ficus maclellandii* 'Alii'
sago palm	*Cycas revoluta*
sansevieria	*Sansevieria* spp.
scented geranium	*Pelargonium* spp.
sensitive plant	*Mimosa pudica*
shamrock	*Oxalis* spp.
shark's fin sansevieria	*Sansevieria masoniana*
'Sharon' begonia	*Begonia* 'Sharon'
'Sharry Baby' oncidium orchid	*Oncidium* 'Sharry Baby'
showy medinilla	*Medinilla magnifica*
Siebold's stonecrop	*Sedum sieboldii*
silver plectranthus	*Plectranthus argentatus*
'Singer's Silver' snake plant	*Sansevieria trifasciata* 'Singer's Silver'
slipper orchid	*Paphiopedilum* spp.
snake plant	*Sansevieria trifasciata*
snowflake aralia	*Trevesia palmata*

COMMON NAME	BOTANICAL NAME
Spanish moss	*Tillandsia usneoides*
spear sansevieria	*Sansevieria cylindrica*
spider plant	*Chlorophytum comosum*
spike moss	*Selaginella* spp.
split-leaf philodendron	*Monstera deliciosa*
Sprengeri fern	*Asparagus densiflorus* Sprengeri Group
staghorn fern	*Platycerium bifurcatum*
starfish cactus	*Stapelia grandiflora*
starfish sansevieria	*Sansevieria cylindrica* 'Boncel'
'Sticks on Fire' pencil cactus	*Euphorbia tirucalli* 'Sticks on Fire'
strawberry firetails	*Acalypha pendula*
strawberry plant	*Fragaria* hybrid
string of bananas	*Senecio radicans*
string of pearls	*Senecio rowleyanus*
sundew	*Drosera* spp.
'Super Atom' philodendron	*Philodendron* 'Super Atom'
'Superclone' sansevieria	*Sansevieria kirkii* 'Superclone'
Surf Song orchid	*Doritaenopsis* 'Kumquat'
Suzanne's euphorbia	*Euphorbia susannae*
Swedish ivy	*Plectranthus ciliatus*
sweet bay laurel	*Laurus nobilis*
Swiss cheese vine	*Monstera obliqua*
'Teardrop' English ivy	*Hedera helix* 'Teardrop'
thimble cactus	*Mammillaria gracilis* var. *fragilis*
ti plant	*Cordyline terminalis*
touch-me-not plant	*Mimosa pudica*
tree houseleek	*Aeonium* spp.
tree ivy	× *Fatshedera lizei*
triangle ficus, triangle fig	*Ficus triangularis*
'Tricolor' fern	*Pteris quadriaurita* 'Tricolor'
'Tricolor' hoya	*Hoya carnosa* 'Tricolor'

COMMON NAME	BOTANICAL NAME
tuberous begonia	*Begonia* Tuberhybrida Group
umbrella tree	*Schefflera actinophylla* 'Amate'
variegated African candelabra cactus	*Euphorbia ammak* var. *variegata*
variegated 'Alii' ficus	*Ficus maclellandii* 'Alii Variegated'
variegated bird's nest sansevieria	*Sansevieria trifasciata* 'Hahnii Variegata'
variegated bottle palm	*Beaucarnea recurvata* 'Gold Star'
variegated Chinese banyan	*Ficus benjamina* 'Variegata'
variegated corncob cactus	*Euphorbia mammillaris* 'Variegata'
variegated dwarf umbrella plant	*Schefflera arboricola* 'Variegata'
variegated fatshedera	× *Fatshedera variegata*
variegated lipstick plant	*Aeschynanthus radicans* 'Variegata'
variegated snake plant	*Sansevieria trifasciata* 'Laurentii'
variegated song of India	*Dracaena reflexa* 'Variegata'
variegated spider plant	*Chlorophytum comosum* 'Variegatum'
Venus flytrap	*Dionaea muscipula*
vriesea bromeliad	*Vriesea ospinae* var. *gruberi*
watch chain	*Crassula muscosa* 'Variegata'
wax begonia	*Begonia* Semperflorens Cultorum Group
wax flower, wax plant	*Hoya* spp.
weeping fig	*Ficus benjamina*
Xanadu philodendron	*Philodendron* 'Winterbourn'
yucca	*Yucca elephantipes*
Zanzibar gem	*Zamioculcas zamiifolia*
zebra plant	*Aphelandra squarrosa*
zygopetalum orchid	*Zygopetalum* spp.
ZZ plant	*Zamioculcas zamiifolia*

RESOURCES

With so many great retailers and artisans out there and more popping up all the time, I couldn't include *all* my favorites here—but below are some of the best and most easily accessible sources for plants, supplies, vessels, and more (and the places where I got much of the product for this book). And be sure to look out for local plant swaps and gatherings, and check out plant societies, botanical gardens, and educational centers in your area—they are filled with excellent information and inspiration.

PLANTS & SUPPLIES

If the plant you've been ogling isn't available in your neck of the woods, check out these online retailers to find new green friends. If your seller is reputable (like those recommended below), your plants will arrive in perfect shape; however, if you order plants, make sure you'll be around when they arrive. Spending more than a few days in a dark box or being left outside in inclement weather isn't good for them.

Black Jungle Terrarium Supply

blackjungleterrariumsupply.com

This supplier offers a wild and wonderful selection of plants, including carnivorous specimens, as well as LED grow lights in various styles.

Brent and Becky's Bulbs

brentandbeckysbulbs.com

Check out this site's indoor bulbs section for some satisfyingly easy blooms to grow from scratch.

Costa Farms

costafarms.com

This company is a wholesaler, meaning consumers can't buy from them (they sell to plant retailers, so you've probably purchased their plants indirectly), but you can learn a lot from their houseplant-focused blog.

Gardener's Supply Co.

gardeners.com

This online garden center has everything! Pick up plants, seeds, potting soil, fertilizer, and extra-large yet lightweight planters.

Kartuz Greenhouse

kartuz.com

The go-to spot for all your begonia needs!

Logee's

logees.com

This company specializes in fruiting, rare, and tropical plants.

Pistils Nursery

pistilsnursery.com

Look to Pistils for hip plants, helpful info, and fine-looking photos to boot.

The Sill

thesill.com

This stylish New York City–based retailer delivers houseplants directly to your door, anywhere in the United States.

VESSELS & PLANT STANDS

Before you go out and buy something new, check out flea markets, garage sales, resale shops, and overstock stores for unconventional vases and hidden gems. Your local hardware store and home goods and design stores (both boutiques and national chains like Pottery Barn and Ikea) are filled with possibilities for vessels, too. Below are some go-to online sources.

Artisans

There is a whole world of talented artisans to explore, including the makers of some of the handcrafted vessels in the book. Search for them online to find out how to get your hands on a piece of their art: All Hands, Aveva Design, Ecoforms, Eric Trine, Esther Pottery, Global Eye Art Collective, Heath Ceramics, Holly Coley, House of Thol, Judy Jackson, Kelly Lamb, Love Fest Fibers, Melanie Abrantes Designs, Michiko Shimada, Modernica, Paige Russell, Pawena, Pseudo Studio, Steel Life, West Perro, and Yonder SF.

Campo de' Fiori

campodefiori.com

When you want to bring an old-world garden feel to the indoors, you can't beat Campo's mossy terra-cotta pots, wrought-iron plants stands, and handblown glass terrariums.

Etsy.com

This online marketplace for makers is a great place to find unique pottery and plant accessories. Shops whose vessels are featured in this book include ArtCraftHome, BrooksideBungalow, CeramicaArtisticaASV, FernandFjord, FreeFolding, IHeartNorwegianWood, OkcinWorkshop, and SaraPaloma.

Ferm Living

fermliving.com

A mecca for all things Danish design, including a fantastic collection of minimalist pots and plant stands (found under the heading "Green Living").

Flying Tiger Copenhagen

flyingtiger.com

Check out this playful store's ever-rotating collection of lighthearted and colorful pieces, at prices that won't empty your wallet.

Kaufmann Mercantile

kaufmann-mercantile.com

From sleek garden tools to brass cachepots, this place has style to spare.

Modern Sprout

modsprout.com

Modern Sprout's delightful goodies include attractive grow lights, mod moss terrariums, and even seed starters and herb kits.

Need Supply Co.

needsupply.com

This clothing and lifestyle brand has a curated collection of out-of-the-ordinary vases and plant stands (look under the "Life" category).

Potted

pottedstore.com

Whether you're looking for a succulent wall planter in the shape of California or a colorful hanging vase, this LA-based store has got you covered. They also host workshops and offer DIY tutorials on their blog.

Terrain

shopterrain.com

Terrain is synonymous with well-made products that bridge the gap between indoors and out. I always end up finding something special from this store, which is a sister company to Anthropologie.

ACKNOWLEDGMENTS

I have such gratitude for the talent, knowledge, and creativity of the whole team involved with the making of this book: First, my editor, Bridget Monroe Itkin, for her guidance, kindness, and expertise down the bookmaking path. Aubrie Pick for having the amazing combination of a down-to-earth demeanor and over-the-top photography skills. Sarah Green, whose behind-the-scenes talent shines throughout the book. My agent, Kitty Cowles, for always steering me in the right direction. Alexis Mersel, for helping get this idea off the ground with eloquence. Molly Watson, for once again transforming my mishmash of words into a cohesive narrative. Lia Ronnen for having the faith to work with me on a second project. The rest of the Artisan team, including Sibylle Kazeroid, Elise Ramsbottom, Paula Brisco, Barbara Peragine, Michelle Ishay-Cohen, Jane Treuhaft, Nancy Murray, Allison McGeehon, Theresa Collier, and Amy Michelson, for all the help along the way. Erin Heimstra and Kate Leonard, for their keen eyes and gift for style. Cortney Munna for managing the shoots and postproduction with clarity and enthusiasm. Tony Colella, Kana Copeland, Bessma Khalaf, and Sherese Elsey, cheers to the finest plant and photo assistants ever. A nod to Sophie de Lignerolles, a talented artist, gardener, and dear friend. And to Shannon Lynn, who pitched in and helped lead Lila B. when an overlapping project needed a pilot.

Thanks also to my friends, colleagues, and neighbors who generously fielded my questions, opened their homes, and lent out their belongings—they are a huge part of what's between these book bindings. To jak.w, who elevated this project when they opened their fabulous studio full of treasures to us. Thank you to Erin Heimstra, Chris Wick, and Benni Amada for allowing us to move into your picturesque home for a few days. To all my neighbors in the Allied Box Factory for putting up with all my green friends that overflowed into our communal hallways and for pitching in when I was searching for the perfect prop. To Granville Greene, Jackie Priestley, and Lawrence Lee for solid advice in your fields of writing, coaching, and horticulture. I feel lucky to have you all in my life! To the folks at Delano Nursery (John, Lauren, Carla, Penny) for not only offering cool plants within the San Francisco Flower Mart but also for loaning me "Phil," your precious 'Jade' pothos. And to Rocket Farms, Costa Farms, Hana Bay Nursery, and the San Francisco Botanical Garden for giving me sound horticultural info. To the talented artists whose artwork dons the walls in this book: Sidnea D'Amico (page 202), John Fraser (page 202), Matthew Frederick (pages 107, 116, 141), Ian Green (page 125), Jennifer Joseph (page 140), Lawrence LaBianca (page 249), Rex Ray (page 248), Melinda Stickney-Gibson (page 111), Myrna Tatar (page 6), and ReChang Tsang (page 193). And finally, a whole bunch of gratitude goes to my sister, Suzanne, who graciously carried the load of our shared endeavors while I concentrated on the book.

INDEX

IN CASE YOU WERE WONDERING . . .

Below I've listed all the plants not otherwise identified that appear in the photographs in this book.

Front cover: TOP SHELF, LEFT TO RIGHT Variegated lipstick plant, *Tillandsia mooreana*, succulents, rex begonia, blue star fern, 'Ruby' earth star, moth orchid; BOTTOM SHELF, LEFT TO RIGHT Asparagus fern, echeveria, rex begonia and 'Kirigami' ornamental oregano, chenille plant, Little Phil philodendron, heart ivy

Page 2: TOP SHELF, LEFT TO RIGHT Glory bower, rex begonia, croton; MIDDLE SHELF, LEFT TO RIGHT Succulents, 'Frizzle Sizzle' albuca, *Pilea peperomioides*; BOTTOM SHELF 'Pink Starlite' earth star; DESKTOP Bonsai ficus; STOOL 'Congo' philodendron

Page 5: LEFT TO RIGHT 'Pink Starlite' earth star and 'Black Mystic' earth star

Page 6: TABLETOP Lavender scallops; HANGING *Tillandsia xerographica*

Page 11: FLOOR, LEFT TO RIGHT Variegated African candelabra cactus, olive, fancy-leaf zonal geranium, 'Colocho' pelargonium, ponytail palm, snowflake aralia; LEFT TO RIGHT, WINDOWSILL 'Sticks on Fire' pencil cactus, paddle plant, golden ball cactus; LEFT TO RIGHT, PLANTER Aloe, aloe, olive, trailing begonia

Page 13: 'Super Atom' philodendron

Page 21: CLOCKWISE FROM TOP LEFT Bunny ears cactus, oxalis (left) and pineapple (right), ZZ plant (left) and metallic palm (right), cupid peperomia

Page 31: LEFT TO RIGHT Chenille plant and red prayer plant

Page 94: CLOCKWISE FROM TOP LEFT Parlor palm, triangle ficus, monstera, rex begonia, spider plant and 'Sharon' begonia

Page 100: Variegated Chinese banyan

Page 120: LEFT TO RIGHT, TOP TO BOTTOM 'Limelight' dracaena, purple waffle plant, parlor palm, ZZ plant

Pages 126–27: FLOOR, LEFT TO RIGHT Napoleon's hat, fiddle-leaf fig, 'Ruby Red' rubber plant, yucca, vriesea bromeliad, copper spoons kalanchoe, billbergia bromeliad; COFFEE TABLE, LEFT TO RIGHT Nerve plant, 'Pink Starlite' earth star and 'Black Mystic' earth star

Pages 134–35: WALL, LEFT TO RIGHT Resurrection plant, *Tillandsia ionantha*, 'Jade' pothos, peperomia; ENTERTAINMENT CENTER, LEFT TO RIGHT 'Sharon' begonia and spider plant, parlor palm, rex begonia; FLOOR, LEFT TO RIGHT Cast iron plant, 'Ruby Red' rubber plant, 'Janet Craig' compacta dracaena, triangle ficus, monstera

Pages 140–41: TOP OF SHELF, LEFT TO RIGHT Variegated Chinese banyan, 'Tricolor' hoya; FIRST SHELF, LEFT TO RIGHT Nerve plant, 'Partita' begonia, Madagascar palm; SECOND SHELF, LEFT TO RIGHT Variegated 'Alii' ficus, Sprengeri fern and China doll, variegated lipstick plant; BOTTOM SHELF, LEFT TO RIGHT

Variegated bird's nest sansevieria, China doll, *Tillandsia xerographica*; FLOOR, LEFT TO RIGHT Variegated bottle palm, nong noch vine, 'Fire' Chinese evergreen

Page 144: HANGING IN WINDOW, LEFT TO RIGHT Jasmine, baby burro's tail, burro's tail, glory bower; WINDOWSILL, LEFT TO RIGHT Artillery plant, thimble cactus; TOP SHELF OF PLANT STAND, LEFT TO RIGHT Mini Hawaiian snow bush, baby burro's tail, tree houseleek, piggyback plant; LEFT TO RIGHT, MIDDLE SHELF OF PLANT STAND *Medinilla* spp., Cape primrose; BOTTOM SHELF OF PLANT STAND Kiwi dragon tree; FLOOR, LEFT TO RIGHT Ming aralia, showy medinilla, Napoleon's hat, variegated dwarf umbrella plant

Pages 146: LEFT TO RIGHT Orange medinilla, metallic palm, Hawaiian snow bush, creeping ficus, variegated Chinese banyan, staghorn fern, 'Bronze Crown' air plant

Page 166: 'Angyo Star' fatshedera

Page 186: TOP TO BOTTOM Goldfish plant, *Tillandsia ionantha*

Pages 190–91: FLOOR, LEFT TO RIGHT 'Ruby Red' rubber plant, Bengal fig, neon pothos, Jack's beanstalk, dwarf umbrella plant, snowflake aralia, 'Dorado' dracaena, golden pothos, croton; TABLE, LEFT TO RIGHT 'Marisela' prayer plant, ivy, 'Amate Soleil' umbrella tree, variegated dwarf umbrella plant, parlor palm; WINDOW Swedish ivy

Page 204: UPPER SHELF Starfish cactus; LOWER SHELF Neon pothos

Page 212: HANGING 'Little Darling' begonia; FLOOR Pothos; BOOKSHELF, TOP TO BOTTOM Starfish cacti, pothos, nerve plant, haworthias, pothos

Page 220: LEFT TO RIGHT Coconut palm, aloe

Page 229: LEFT OF TUB Madagascar dragon tree; RIGHT OF TUB, CLOCKWISE FROM TOP LEFT 'Congo' philodendron, monstera, variegated snake plant, 'Tricolor' hoya, 'Tricolor' fern, bird's nest sansevieria; SHELF Spider plant

Page 236: TABLETOP *Tillandsia ionantha*; LEFT PANEL, LEFT TO RIGHT Clumping *Tillandsia ionantha*, *Tillandsia ionantha*; RIGHT PANEL, CLOCKWISE FROM TOP LEFT *Tillandsia ionantha*, Spanish moss, *Tillandsia xerographica*

Page 241: TOP SHELF Glory bower; THIRD SHELF, LEFT TO RIGHT Red prayer plant, kangaroo ivy, peperomia, rex begonia, croton; FOURTH SHELF, LEFT TO RIGHT *Pilea peperomioides*, croton, succulents, 'Frizzle Sizzle' albuca, *Pilea peperomioides*; FIFTH SHELF, LEFT TO RIGHT *Tillandsia tectorum*, pixie peperomia cutting, 'Pink Starlite' earth star; DESKTOP, LEFT TO RIGHT Ti plant cuttings, succulents, flaming Katy, bonsai ficus; CHEST mistletoe fig; STOOL 'Congo' philodendron

Page 258: LEFT TO RIGHT, TABLETOP Panda plant; 'Ming Thing' cactus; hairy-fruited wickerwork cactus, crested elkhorn, and Suzanne's euphorbia; FLOOR Snake plant